LOUISIANA STATE UNIVERSITY STUDIES

Max Goodrich, General Editor

Social Science Series
Walter C. Richardson, Editor

Number Thirteen
Negro Troops of Antebellum Louisiana:
A History of the Battalion of Free Men of Color

Negro Troops
of Antebellum
Louisiana

A HISTORY OF
THE BATTALION OF FREE MEN OF
COLOR

Roland C. McConnell

LOUISIANA STATE UNIVERSITY PRESS / Baton Rouge

TO ISABEL

ACKNOWLEDGMENTS

In the preparation of this book, I am indebted to many individuals. The staff members of the Library of Congress, the National Archives, the New Orleans Public Library, the Louisiana State Museum, the Louisiana State Archives, the Enoch Pratt Free Library of Baltimore, and the libraries of Louisiana State University, Tulane University, Howard University, Johns Hopkins University, Peabody Institute, and Morgan State College placed the useful materials and facilities of their institutions at my disposal. The Right Reverend Bernard Herman, O.M.I., St. Louis Cathedral, New Orleans, and Miss Mary M. Impastato, secretary of the cathedral, permitted my use of the archives of that church. The Adjutant General of Louisiana authorized the use of the Military Collection of Jackson Barracks, and Thomas Harrison, the military historian, furnished me with valuable information including the specially prepared notes on Fort St. Leon.

Walter Goldstein of New Orleans provided me with information on weapons and uniforms used in Louisiana during the period. John Crawford and Barthelmy Roussève, both of New Orleans, arranged for me to meet and interview many of the nominal descendants of the early Negro soldiers. Mrs. Naomi Drake, Bureau of Vital Statistics, City of New Orleans Health Department, furnished me with certain information of value.

Israel Wice made available to me certain collections in the office of the chief of military history of the United States Army. Dr. Roscoe Hill helped me obtain certain information concerning the colored militia from the archives in Seville, Spain. Manuel Romero Gomez, of Seville, furnished me with transcripts from the *Archivo General de Indias* there.

I wish to thank the officials of the Mississippi Department of Archives and History for permission to reprint portions from the *Mississippi Provincial Archives*, edited and translated by Dunbar Rowland and A. G. Sanders, and *The Letter Books of W. C. C. Claiborne*, edited by Dunbar Rowland; Mrs. Caroline M. Burson for permission to quote from *The Stewardship of Don Esteban Miró, 1782–1792*; and Barthelmy Rousséve, who allowed me to quote from *The Negro in Louisiana*.

I am also grateful to the Louisiana Historical Society, the Southern Historical Society, and the Association for the Study of Negro Life and History for the use of their collections and for materials published in their journals.

I am indebted to Professor Welfred Holmes of Morgan State College, who carefully read the complete manuscript and gave valuable suggestions; to Professor Benjamin Quarles for his expert assistance on portions of the study; and to Professor Ulysses Lee of the same faculty and Dr. Harold Pinkett of the National Archives for their helpful comments. To Professor Jane de Grummond of Louisiana State University, whose suggestions were very useful, I also wish to extend my appreciation.

Morgan State College granted me a sabbatical leave for this study for which I am grateful, as I am to the Board of Research and Publication of that institution for a grant-in-aid of research. For making this publication possible, along with suggestions and encouragement on the way, I owe a special debt of gratitude to the Louisiana State University Press. Finally to my wife, who throughout the entire work has given me unstintingly of her time, continous help, and constant encouragement, I am indebted beyond expression.

With such bountiful assistance it would seem that this work should have no imperfections. But it probably does. For them I am completely responsible.

Roland C. McConnell
Baltimore, Maryland

PREFACE

PRIOR TO THE CIVIL WAR whenever Louisiana—whether as a province, territory, or state—was endangered, Negro troops were used for its security. Beginning as slave soldiers under the French, these troops emerged as a Battalion of Free Men of Color under the Spanish and culminated their services under Andrew Jackson in the Battle of New Orleans.

The existence of such a corps alone justifies an account of its history. Indeed, the battalion is unique in American history. It was organized in the Deep South during the period of American slavery, and, of equal significance, within the shadow of Haiti during the revolution there. In addition, the development and utilization of the corps furnished a number of precedents which were followed in the subsequent organization and use of Negro troops in the United States.

That the struggle of the corps to maintain its identity and status was at times almost an overwhelming one is not disputed. As the events unfold, one wonders not so much at what these troops did, but that they were a reality and for so long.

CONTENTS

Negro Troops of Antebellum Louisiana

CHAPTER I

BEGINNINGS UNDER THE FRENCH

"... as sons of freedom you are called upon to defend our most inestimable blessing. As Americans, your Country looks with confidence to her adopted Children for a Valorous support, ... —As fathers, husbands, and Brothers, you are summoned to rally around the standard of the Eagle, to defend all which is dear in existence." [1] Thus with these words, Andrew Jackson in his address, "To the Free Coloured Inhabitants of Louisiana" urged the Negro to fight the British on the eve of the Battle of New Orleans in 1814. This was only one of several occasions when Negroes were called upon to help save Louisiana from an enemy. In 1729, when total destruction first threatened the little French colony, their help was needed. This marked the first significant service by the Negro in the defense of Louisiana.

At that time there were about two thousand Negro slaves in the colony (more than a third of its population) scattered throughout the settlement along the Mississippi River from the Gulf of Mexico to Illinois.[2] Most of them were concentrated in the lower part of Louisiana, especially in and around New Orleans, the little capital just emerging from the mud on the first prominent bend of the Mississippi a little over a hundred miles from its mouth. Nearly all of these slaves had been brought from French West Africa by the *Compagnie des Indies* (Company of the Indies), the giant commercial company which monopolized the development of Louisiana, including its slavery and slave trade, from 1718 to 1731. With the exception of those retained by the Company, the slaves were sold to the settlers, outright or on time, to be used in the cultivation of tobacco on plantations near New Or-

3

leans and around the military posts up and down the river.[3] The Company kept a hundred or more slaves for use in public works in and around New Orleans and on its plantation nearby.[4] Some it assigned to work at posts like Natchez, about one hundred and seventy miles above New Orleans on the bluffs overhanging the Mississippi. Certain slaves of both the settlers and the Company were classified *piece d'inde* by the organization and given a fixed value at the time of their arrival. They had to be in good health, aged seventeen and above, presumably not over thirty if male, and fifteen to thirty if female.[5]

The status of all these Negroes was fixed by the *Code Noir*, 1724, which, in addition to its conventional restrictive features necessary to slavery, made them Catholics and provided for their welfare in a manner enlightened for the time.[6] Slaves were to be administered the sacraments of baptism and marriage in the Roman Catholic church, and they were to be buried according to the ritual of the Church. Slave families were not to be broken nor slave children sold before age fourteen. If slaves were ill treated by their masters, they could report their owners to certain officials of the colony, and if brought to trial they could appeal a case to the Superior Court. Provision of adequate food and clothing, and care during illness and in old age were specified in the code. Nor were slaves to be denied the use of Sundays and holidays entirely for themselves.

Freed slaves were to be granted the same privileges and immunities enjoyed by persons born free. Avenues to freedom included self-purchase, meritorious deeds, will or wish of the master, and tutoring his children. Racial admixture, which the code prohibited, was realistically recognized by the term *gens de couleur*, people of color. Although only six persons of mixed parentage were listed in the census of 1732, a social tendency toward miscegenation began in the frontier community where French and other European women were scarce. This continued throughout the period of slavery, and in time the resulting mixed group outnumbered the nonwhite group in lower Louisiana (especially in and around New Orleans).

In addition to the *Code Noir,* the hundred or more slaves of the Company were further regulated by a special set of rules and practices drawn up mainly by Sieur Louis Prat, surgeon, councillor, and medical inspector of the Company. Considerably enlightened regulations were concerned with the health of slaves as well as their skills and organization. According to the health regimen, slaves were encouraged to marry but forbidden to abandon their wives, and prospective mothers were to receive special care.[7] Slaves were to be worked moderately but kept busy, fed and clothed properly, provided with proper bedding, afforded opportunities to bathe, cared for when ill, and shown appreciation.

It became Company practice by 1728 to place selected Negroes as apprentices with the best French craftsmen.[8] This was done because white workmen were scarce and expensive. At the same time a constant supply of skilled workmen was assured, as the Company exercised the right of first choice of slaves from the newly arrived slave ships and their subsequent assignment.

Finally, Negroes belonging to the Company were organized into semimilitary units for control purposes; slaves who were thought to be dependable and who had leadership qualities were placed over these units.[9] Whenever possible, Senegalese were appointed to such positions, for it was believed that their mental endowment enabled them to learn a trade quickly or serve in the house efficiently and gave them an innate ability to command other Negroes. In such roles they were found to be competent, faithful, and appreciative, and their importation was particularly urged. It was to this group of slaves that Governor Étienne Périer turned for support in the wake of the Natchez massacre in 1729.

The Natchez Indians, enraged at continuing encroachments upon their land by the commander at Fort Rosalie, the post which protected the little French settlement at Natchez, laid plans to wipe out the entire French colony. Promised the aid of the neighboring Yazoos, Natchitoches, and Chickasaws, the Natchez suddenly attacked the French settlement on November 28, 1729, and began a massacre which eventually spread to the Yazoo and threatened other posts along the Mississippi.

The Natchez killed well over two hundred settlers, among whom there were many women and children. They took many captives, including two Frenchmen (a wagoner and a tailor, for their skills in the service of the tribe) and two hundred slaves whom they planned to sell later to the English in the Carolinas. Some few slaves who joined the Natchez against the French were promised their freedom. Then, as a final act of destruction, the Natchez reduced the entire settlement to ashes, including 200,000 pounds of tobacco which were to be shipped to France as the main money crop. Only twelve Indians were killed in the carnage.

From Natchez alone not more than twenty-six persons, including five or six slaves most of whom were wounded, managed to escape from the post. Three of these slaves, with other survivors, eventually reached New Orleans and furnished the Governor with details of the disaster.[10]

Governor Périer was unprepared for such an emergency. Concentrating on the cultivation of tobacco to make the colony prosperous, he had adopted a policy of increasing the importation of slaves and giving large quantities of French merchandise as gifts to the Indians to assure their peace and friendship.[11] In so doing, however, he had neglected military defense—not only was New Orleans unfortified but the shortage of military personnel was critical. Of some four hundred soldiers scattered throughout the colony, only sixty men were healthy enough to march. Furthermore, there were few officers upon whom the Governor could depend for vigorous action and none, he admitted regretfully, in his dispatch to the French colonial minister, "on whom I can count to command in my absence." [12] Meanwhile, the massacre was spreading northward to the Yazoo and westward toward the Natchitoches. "Frenchmen are being killed everywhere without one post being able to help another," Périer lamented to the minister.[13]

Nevertheless, the Governor took immediate action, deciding to do the best with what he had. His strategy involved containment of the massacre as well as an offensive against the Natchez. He called on all available manpower, including the slaves of the Company. He dispatched volunteer messengers to alert the distant posts up the Mississippi as far as the Illinois River. On this assignment he utilized the services of a few of the braver Negro slaves, promising them their freedom in return for courageous and faithful service.[14]

On December 3, Périer ordered the destruction of the Chaouacha Indians, a small tribe located below the capital, as a warning to other Indian tribes near New Orleans who might join the conspiracy, and to allay the fear of the inhabitants of the city and vicinity. He assigned the task to the Negro volunteers of the Company who, using knives and sharp-edged weapons, executed their mission of death with "as much promptness as secrecy." [15] Few Indians were left—only those who escaped or who were absent at the time. This act had its desired effect; not only did other little tribes nearby maintain a respectful attitude from then on but the colonists began to act more fearlessly. Périer was so impressed with the efficiency of his slave soldiers that he contemplated using more of them to destroy other such potential Indian enemies. But when he considered the possibility of their joining the Indians, as had certain slaves at Natchez, he dismissed the idea for the time being. On December 15 the Governor sent a pirogue manned by twenty volunteers, six of whom were Negroes, to carry powder to the Illinois posts and pick up any voyageurs on the way and return them to New Orleans.[16]

The Governor's action was not without merit. He had alerted some posts and reopened communications between them and New Orleans. He had partially secured New Orleans by creating bad blood between black and red men which he hoped would discourage further alliances between the two groups against the French. But he had not yet halted the massacre.[17] The Yazoos attacked the post of that name early in January. Most of the inhabitants, including the small garrison at Fort St. Claude designed to protect the post, were killed and the post was then burned. Similarly, the Natchitoches attacked the post of that name in their territory but because of the vigilance of its commander were unsuccessful.

Later the Governor distributed arms to 150 colonists of New Orleans who were organized into four companies, and to 15 Negroes. With these and other reinforcements an attack lasting from February 12 through February 26, 1730, was made against the Natchez near Pointe Coupée under the direction of Sieur Henry de Louboey. Although the French were unable to destroy the Natchez at this time they were successful in recovering fifty-four French women and children and about one hundred slaves. These had been taken from the Natchez by the Choctaws, then allied to the French, in an engagement on January 27, 1730.

Even though Périer's official report to the ministry of the colonies listed the weaknesses of the troops as the first reason for his failure to conquer the Natchez, he praised the colonists for serving with distinction. In the same communication, he commented that "the Negroes to the number of fifteen who were permitted to take up arms did deeds of surprising valor." And he added with mixed feelings: ". . . if these soldiers had not been so expensive and so necessary to the colony it would have been safer to use them [the slave soldiers]" instead of the French soldiers who were so ineffective.[18]

Jacques De la Chaise, president of the Superior Council of Louisiana, was pleased with the overall performance of the Negroes in the Natchez affair. He considered their record commendable, not only in fighting and communications, but for the obvious bravery displayed by those who died at the sides of their masters. Of such calibre were the slaves of the Charente family, who lost their lives in the Natchez massacre, and the Negro of the Jesuit Father Souel at Yazoo, who was reported burned at the stake with his master.[19]

With the bravery and loyalty of the Negroes in mind, De la Chaise drafted a memorial (early in 1730) to the members of the Superior Council in which he pointed out the importance to the French of attaching and holding the Negroes in such a manner that they could be relied on in such crises. He strongly recommended freedom for all slaves who had risked their lives for the French. In addition, he proposed that "a company be formed of free Negroes" which could be assigned to strategic posts by the commander and which would always be "ready to march at short notice." [20] All such action which might be taken had to adhere to the slave code.

M. De la Chaise died sometime before January 6, 1730, and it is impossible to determine accurately if and when he presented his memorial to the Superior Council, as it is dated posthumously May 16, 1730.[21] However, François Fleuriau, attorney general and member of the Council, as well as a close advisor of the former president, presented a similar proposition to that body on May 13, of the same year.[22] It is possible that Fleuriau, who was responsible for the inventory of the effects of De la Chaise, which included many documents and papers—some badly charred—borrowed the ideas for his recommendations from an examination of these papers, or he might have been carrying out a request of De la Chaise. At any rate, the Attorney General also urged freedom for those Negroes whom officers' reports had proved loyally useful to the French and recommended the formation of a military company from these men for instant call. Moreover, Fleuriau advocated the immediate fulfillment of the promise of freedom and appended a list of names of candidates for emancipation.

Some slaves like Negro Ticou or Dicou (later François Ticou), "of the Senegal nation," were freed for bravery in the war.[23] But the idea of forming a company of free Negroes did not immediately materialize, for the question of expediency complicated the matter. It was known that there were some Negro accomplices in the massacre at the Natchez post who had joined the Indians in order to secure their freedom. The failure of the Choctaw allies to destroy the Natchez in the December attack had been due, in part, to the resistance of captured Negro slaves, who had not only prevented the Choctaws from seizing a quantity of gunpowder, but also had joined in combat against them.[24]

Moreover, in 1730 when the Governor had almost completed plans

for a second movement against the Natchez and was awaiting reinforcements from France, a slave plot was discovered. Samba, a desperate Bambara Negro, and eight others (principally from his African
home) were leaders in the plot. Samba's relationship with whites had
been a stormy and unique one. He had resisted the French in Africa,
and had attempted a mutiny on board the slave ship enroute to America, but after arrival had accepted Christianity, had learned to speak
French, and was made a commander of the Negroes in New Orleans
belonging to the Company of the Indies.[25]

The plans of the conspirators called for slaves in and around New
Orleans to put their masters to death after they had retired for the
night, seize their weapons, take over New Orleans and eventually the
whole colony.[26] A sort of Bambara republic was then to be set up
which was to be governed by members of that nation through a system
of rotation of office. But freedom was not to be universal; Negroes not
of that nation were to be kept as slaves.

As a result of an investigation which grew out of a chance remark
made by a Negro slave woman, the plot was discovered and the leaders
apprehended. Tried and sentenced to death, eight men including Samba were broken on the wheel, and one woman was hanged.[27] This, the
first major slave conspiracy in lower Louisiana, following close on the
heels of the massacre, if successful, would have been calamitous to the
new colony. Nevertheless, Samba had introduced into the colony a
plague, endemic to slavery—the slave conspiracy—with which the authorities and citizens would continuously grapple. And it would affect
the development of the Negro troops throughout the entire course of
their history.

The conspiracy and Negro-Indian alliances estranged Périer from
all Negroes in the colony. It was not until some of the Company's Negroes, whom he had threatened to hang as conspirators, voluntarily
attacked and defeated the remaining Chaouacha Indians that they
were redeemed in his eyes.[28]

Affairs in New Orleans were sufficiently settled by late December in
1730 to allow Périer's army, then composed of reinforcements from
France, regular troops of the colony, and the militia, to move against
the Natchez. Proceeding up the Red River to the Black River and up the
Black some distance to what was then the Silver River, they found
the Natchez stronghold on January 21, 1731, near what is now the
town of Trinity in Catahoula Parish.[29] The attack lasted off and on
until the twenty-fifth when the Natchez surrendered. At that time, the

French wagoner and tailor, a number of women and children, and many Negroes were rescued. That night, however, most of the Natchez braves escaped after a sally which surprised the French.

Périer does not indicate how many Negroes participated in this engagement. It is known, however, that on the first day of combat a Negro was killed and a militia officer was wounded.[30] Earlier, as part of the same campaign, an armed party composed of twenty Indians and free Negroes whom Périer had sent in a large pirogue to the fort at Natchez, hastily erected since the November massacre, was attacked on its way. Most of them were killed or wounded.

Meanwhile in Paris on January 23, 1731, the directors of the Company of the Indies, already suffering heavy financial losses in the promotion of the Louisiana colony and now completely discouraged by the Natchez massacre and the slave revolt almost unanimously decided to return the colony to the King. By November 15, 1731, the retrocession was effected and the colony became Crown.[31]

When the Crown acquired the colony, Louis XV received some 150 slaves, most of them skilled, who were employed in a brick kiln and on a plantation of the Company located across the river from New Orleans. Shortly thereafter some fifty or more additional slaves were acquired from the Company. These slaves helped to man and service the vessels of the Company which now became part of the King's fleet.[32]

The Crown also inherited the troublesome problem of the subjection of the Indians. The Natchez had not been completely broken, and they not only continued to harass the French colonists but had been joined by the powerful and warlike Chickasaws who had given them asylum. The fact that Périer had sold two of the Natchez head men, the Sun and Little Sun, into slavery at Santo Domingo, angered the Natchez additionally. Moreover, the suspicious actions of the Choctaws, allies of the French, raised doubts about their loyalty and dependability. For his overall administration, especially his Indian policy, Périer was recalled shortly after the retrocession.

He was replaced in 1733 by Jean Baptiste le Moyne, Sieur de Bienville, his predecessor. Bienville, founder of New Orleans in 1718, had been governor and commandant general of Louisiana at various times between 1702–23, and was a successful Indian fighter. From the very outset, the new Governor decided to make war on the Chickasaws. Knowledge that the English were attempting to induce the Choctaws to make peace with the Chickasaws, protectors of the Natchez, made this action imperative.

The main difficulty confronting him was an old one—the weakness of his military forces. There were only thirteen companies of from thirty-five to forty soldiers each in all of Louisiana at Bienville's disposal.[33] These were distributed in such a manner that it was impossible to bring them together without exposing the several outlying posts to danger. Three were at Fort Chartres near Kaskaskia, far to the north in the Illinois Country; one each was at Natchez, Natchitoches, and Balize; four were at New Orleans with detachments upriver at Pointe Coupée and the Tunicas, including a Swiss company of mercenaries; and three were far to the east at Mobile.

The troops immediately available to Bienville from the capital totaled only two hundred, a number insufficient to deal with the five hundred men of the Chickasaws and the Natchez. Unless he were sent a sufficient number of recruits, Bienville felt he would have to raise three hundred militiamen from among the colonists, despite their protests.

Although sixteen companies were scattered throughout New Orleans in 1735, their total strength was reduced by the loss of 142 soldiers through death, desertion, or other causes, and by the large number who were sick. Meanwhile, not only had Indian relations become strained, but each day brought the increasing threat of war from the combined Chickasaws and Natchez while the Indian allies of the French—the Choctaws—became increasingly neutral.

The Governor, intent on getting the war under way, informed the colonial minister that "for want of soldiers I shall send out militia and even Negroes in order to be at least on an equality with our enemies." [34] He added that he realized this was an unpopular decision in a colony so hard put for agricultural workers as Louisiana, yet he emphasized that the necessity of the times justified such a measure, and hoped that His Lordship would not disapprove. His plans called for the campaign against the Chickasaws to start from Mobile.

By April 1, 1736, Bienville had assembled his forces at Fort Condé at Mobile. They were composed of 604 men, nine companies of French troops of 30 men each and 35 officers, two militia and one volunteer company of 150 men and 9 officers. In addition there were 140 Negroes, both slave and free.[35] Of these, the free Negroes comprised a small unit or cadre for a company. Some of the slaves, either selected or to be selected, were promised their freedom for risking their lives in the service of the King. Between April 23 and 26 at Fort Tombecbee (near present-day Epps in Sumter County) the jumping-off point and place of rendezvous with the Choctaw chiefs, Bienville reviewed his troops. At this time, he also formed a company of 45 armed Negroes over which he set free Negroes as officers, a move unprecedented in the affairs of the colony.[36]

Bienville left Fort Tombècbee on May 3 but was slowed by the rainy season so that he did not reach the village of the Chickasaws until the twenty-fifth. The attack by his forces against the enemy on a well-fortified hill was unsuccessful. Two officers were killed, five were wounded, and the casualties among the enlisted men were proportional. The Negroes who had to place the mantlets (movable screens from behind which the French soldiers fired) panicked when one of their men was killed and another wounded. They fled, leaving the screens behind.[37]

The conduct of the company of Negroes under fire was unbecoming even though that was its first such exposure. Only the bravery of Simon, a free man and captain of the Negro company, enabled it to escape censorship. Instead of quitting the battlefield when his men fled, he stood his ground and remained exposed with the French officers and men until further orders.[38]

Meanwhile, Bienville, observing his troops falling back and learning of apparent enemy reinforcements from the flank, ordered a retreat and the rescue of the casualties which numbered some thirty-five dead and fifty-two wounded.[39]

Sometime after retreat that day, Captain Simon further distinguished himself by an exceptionally bold feat performed before the whole army. Starting at a run to the height on which the enemy fort was located, he continued "though the Indians sallied out and balls were raining around him" [40] until he reached a group of horses at pasture. He then selected a fine mare, sprang on her back, and rode to camp unscratched. The ovation for his bold act was tremendous. The act itself, though dangerous, doubtless was performed by Simon in order to restore confidence among his troops, as well as to gain esteem for black soldiers in the eyes of the French. This it did and perhaps more. It may have contributed to the assurance of freedom for the slave soldiers of the company—in its next mission the following year it functioned as a free company.

Blaming the shortage of military personnel and equipment and the conduct of officers and soldiers for the failure of his first campaign, Bienville urged upon the ministry the necessity of another move against the Chickasaws. He made it clear, however, that without increased supplies and adequate reinforcements such a campaign would fail. The ministry, after due consideration, decided to continue the war and ordered Bienville to prepare another expedition. Reinforcements, including 550 fully equipped soldiers of the marine and a detachment of artillery and miners, were to be sent from France. Volunteer troops and Indians from Canada and the Illinois Country were also to join him. However, Sieur de Noailles D'Aimé, a naval captain accompanying the troops from France, was to be immediate commander of all troops of the expedition although under the orders of the Governor.[41]

On April 30, 1739, Bienville sent a preliminary detachment of three officers, seventy soldiers, and twenty Negroes up the Mississippi. Near what is now Memphis they located a suitable landing place where supplies could be collected and from which a large army could be launched.[42]

After many months of preparations, the troops moved out of New Orleans. The vanguard under Jean Baptiste de Noyan, Bienville's nephew, left in time to reach the general rendezvous near Memphis by August. It was followed by the main body under Sieur de Noailles, while the rear guard under Bienville left the city on September 12, 1739.

In November, 1739, Bienville commanded over 2,500 troops at the recently completed Fort Assumption near present-day Memphis. They, in part, were composed of 129 officers, 1,066 soldiers, 536 Indians, and 270 Negroes, all of whom had come up from New Orleans and its vicinity. Included within the number of Negroes according to Fontaine Meine, an officer in the expedition who listed its military components, were *"50 négres libres"* who composed the company of free Negroes.[43] In addition there were 166 Frenchmen, including officers, and 328 Indians from Canada, and 220 Indians from the Illinois Country.

Even though a regular company of free Negroes had become a reality, most of the Negroes in this expedition were slaves requisitioned from settlers. Bienville informed the ministry that he had made a levy of nearly three hundred Negroes among the inhabitants who were exempted from serving personally in this expedition. This was in keeping with his announced policy of disturbing the colonists in their work as little as possible.[44] Too, he felt that most of the colonists could not withstand the fatigue of the long journey and the rigors of the campaign. Many colonists, however, accompanied the expedition.

The Negroes helped relieve the soldiers of the marine, many of whom had become hospitalized in New Orleans before the expedition started, while others became ill afterward. In fact, camp casualties from illness and death became so great early in 1740 that Bienville's call for service was answered mainly from the red men and black men of his troops.[45]

Apart from death, illness, and fatigue, another obstacle which soon confronted the expedition was rainy weather, which completely broke down Bienville's logistics. Not only did he lose many horses, cattle, and supplies, but muddy and inundated roads prevented transportation of the heavy weapons thought so necessary to the success of the expedition. Because of these adversities, Bienville called a council of war at Fort Assumption on February 8, 1740, to discuss the advisability of carrying on the campaign against odds that might compromise the King's arms. A week later, after a series of conferences, he decided to discontinue the campaign.[46] Preparations for the return march were completed, and Bienville departed for New Orleans, April 1, 1740. This brought to a close the last of the series of French expeditions against the Indians in which Negroes participated. For the most part both the enslaved and the freed had given a good account of themselves and proved their loyalty to the French. At the same time, they had acquired valuable military and disciplinary experience. This military service provided an avenue to freedom for the enslaved. And for the free, definitely organized into a company with their own officers by the second Chickasaw War, there was the rewarding knowledge that the government also depended upon them for its defense against a common enemy. Here was the nucleus of a colored militia with an experience and tradition that would serve Louisiana well in the future.

Of significance, too, is the fact that freedom for the American Negro in Louisiana from the very beginning was based largely on his military service; fifty or more Negroes of New Orleans had replaced slavery with freedom earned at the risk of their lives on the battlefield. France had risked arming the Negro slave and making him a soldier, a chance born in necessity but based in part on confidence. Those Negroes selected had not abused this trust but made the most of it. And crowning all of this was the simple fact that Negroes helped save Louisiana from destruction by the Natchez and the Chickasaw Indians, the colony's first formidable enemies.

CHAPTER II

IN THE SERVICE OF SPAIN

NEGRO TROOPS of Louisiana saw their next service in the American Revolution as militiamen fighting for Spain under the command of Bernardo de Gálvez. Spain had acquired New Orleans and that part of Louisiana west of the Mississippi from France in 1762 for supporting her in the Seven Years War. In 1779 Spain was again France's ally and launched an offensive against the British from Louisiana in which this militia saw action.

That a militia could be formed from the able bodied free men of color in New Orleans at that time reflected not only the increase in number of the free people of color there but also their emergence as a separate and distinct class in addition to the conventional white and slave groups. This class, recognized as a third one in New Orleans and Louisiana during the Spanish administration, was composed of two streams: (1) free Negroes who had acquired their freedom through acts of bravery, as in the Indian war under the French, or through self-purchase (manumission) or as descendants of free Negroes; and (2) people of mixed blood who had received their freedom because of a special relationship with their masters, especially Spanish masters who had freed their colored offspring. This free Negro population increased not only through their own procreation but also as a result of a pattern of cohabitation of Spanish officials with women of color, which became legalized and institutionalized for Spaniards of rank in spite of the *Code Noir,* which they had inherited. Judge Isaac T. Preston, in the Badillo Case of 1851 involving the cohabitation of a free woman of color with a Spanish officer for fifty years and the subsequent property rights after his

15

death, aptly explains the arrangement which contributed to the increase and emergence of the free people of color as a class.[1] "By an express law of the *Partidas*," whose origin may be traced to the administration of Spain by the Roman Empire, "the governors of the provinces," according to the judge, "were forbidden to marry, and authorized to have concubines . . . ." This became the law of Louisiana under the Spanish. Since "there were in the colony but few women of the white race and hardly any of equal condition with the officers of the Government and troops . . . the inevitable consequence was . . . connection with women of color. This custom, coming as it did from the ruling class, soon spread throughout the colony . . ." and became the leading source for manumissions in Louisiana.[2]

The formation of the Negro militia also revealed the impact of Spain's reorganizational policy concerning imperial defenses as a result of her poor showing against the English in the Seven Years War —especially the loss of the so-called impregnable Havana, key to New Spain, which was returned by the peace settlements. Projected in 1762, the new scheme reorganized, among other troops, the ancient militia of color of Havana into a company called free *pardos* of lighter-skinned Negroes who ranged from mulattoes to those who escaped detection by color.[3] This company had a strength of eighty men commanded by a subinstructor, a chief instructor, and four veteran instructors. To this outfit, which served as a pattern, a newly organized company of free *morenos,* or darker Negroes who ranged from near mulatto to black, was to be added.[4] By 1769 not only had the measures been carried out where possible in the Caribbean area, but Alesandro O'Reilly, lieutenant general of the infantry, who was a key figure in the reorganization, carried the two newly organized colored companies from Havana with other troops to New Orleans when he went there in August of that year to subject the province to the obedience of the King after a moribund revolution.[5]

Although O'Reilly organized four companies of white militiamen before returning with his troops to Cuba in December of 1770, he was unable to do more than furnish, through the colored militia from Havana, a pattern for such an organization in New Orleans in the future. The number of able-bodied free colored men in New Orleans was insufficient for a regulation company at the time as it amounted to only sixty-two free colored males of all ages in New Orleans in 1771.[6] Yet O'Reilly was too able an officer to leave all to chance and partially assured the emergence of a colored militia by two measures. He contributed to the potential Negro manpower by freeing, in many cases at the request of French officers and civilians who were leaving the colony at the changeover, numbers of those held in bondage, especially slave mothers and their offspring of mixed parentage.[7] At the same time, for administrative purposes, he transferred Louisiana to the Captain General of Cuba, with headquarters at Havana, thus making regulations concerning the colored militia there applicable in New Orleans.

By the time Spain declared war against Britain in the American Revolution all the essential elements for a Negro militia were present in New Orleans: authorization, organizational format, and manpower in the form of 169 free colored males, of whom ninety-two were mulattoes or of mixed blood and seventy-seven were darker Negroes.[8] To Bernardo de Gálvez fell the lot of organizing and using his corps against the British.

Gálvez, member of a well-to-do family prominent in Spanish imperial affairs, governor of Louisiana and colonel of the permanent regiment of New Orleans, was assigned the responsibility of directing the operations against the British two years after his arrival in the capital. His overall objective was to drive them from the Gulf of Mexico and the banks of the Mississippi. To accomplish this he was to organize as soon as possible an expedition of whatever land and sea forces were available, attack Mobile and Pensacola, the keys to the Gulf of Mexico, and either before or afterwards the British posts on the Mississippi.[9] Gálvez decided to attack first the British posts. By August 2, 1779, he had begun a recruitment program and within two weeks had enlisted a sufficient number of whites and Negroes to march against the enemy on the twenty-third. His little army was unable to set out against the British until four days later because of a devastating hurricane.

His forces consisted of 500 veteran troops, including 370 from Mexico and the Canary Islands and 130 whose source is not given; 20 carabiniers, 60 militiamen and inhabitants, and 80 free Negroes and mulattoes from New Orleans; Oliver Pollock, agent of Virginia and of the Continental Congress, 2 officers, and 7 Americans, who were also in the city; a total of 670 "men of all species, nations and colors," with a sick artillery officer and without an engineer.[10]

The eighty free Negroes of New Orleans whom Gálvez enlisted were organized by him into two companies classified as nearly as possible by color, one made up of dark Negroes and the other one of men of lighter complexion. The superior officer was white, but other officers were colored, whose assignment also followed the color line.

Enroute to Manchac, the first British post on the river against which an attack was planned, they were joined by 600 men of every class and color from the German and Acadian coasts and other points and by 160 Indian volunteers. In the order of march the Negroes and Indians led as scouts, followed by regular troops and the militia. Gálvez reported that sickness and fatigue reduced his forces to a third of the total 1,430, so that he had only about 475 effectives.

Arriving at Fort Bute de Manchac on September 7, the Spanish surprised and captured the installation, taking a captain, a lieutenant, and eighteen men prisoners. The bulk of the English troops had left for Baton Rouge, a few miles away, against which Gálvez moved his troops after a few days' rest. Baton Rouge was too well defended and heavily fortified to be taken by assault. Battery emplacements were built for siege tactics, while a false attack in which the colored troops were used was made from another position. On September 21, 1779, after three and a half hours of heavy firing the fort was dismantled and the English garrison surrendered.[11] The surrender terms included Fort Pamure at Natchez. Previously, a small fort on the Amite River and another on Thompson's Creek were surrendered by the British.

Meanwhile, Lake Pontchartrain and nearby waters were rid of English vessels by an American privateer and a Spanish vessel.

The success of Gálvez and his little army was phenomenal. They had freed the Mississippi River of the English flag, captured some five hundred veteran troops and a few hundred white militiamen and Negroes, with one soldier killed and two wounded. Both Gálvez and his ministry were most laudatory in their praise of the troops. *La Gazeta de Madrid,* on January 14, 1780, issued a semi-official report of the war as a supplement to the regular edition. In praising the militia and other individual units, Gálvez did not fail to mention the colored troops. "No less deserving of eulogy are the companies of Negroes and free Mulattoes," his citation read, "who were continually occupied in the outposts, in false attacks, and discoveries, exchanging shots with the enemy" and who he pointed out, "conducted themselves with as much valor and generosity as the white." [12]

In citing individuals, the following line officers of the colored units were named: Simon Calfat, captain of the Negroes and mulattoes, who was white and owner of a considerable number of slaves, some whom he hired out and others whom he freed; and Bautista Ogon (Hagon) and Felipe Ruben, lieutenants; Francisco Drovuill (Dorville), Noel

Carrière, Bacus Nichols, and Luis la Nuit, sublieutenants, each of whom was nonwhite. To each of these His Spanish Majesty gave a medal in addition to pay as reward for his performance.[13]

The background of these Negro commissioned officers is obscure, although they all were of slave descent. Carrière, who became prominent in the colored militia, was connected through slavery to a French settler of the same name who was established in Louisiana by 1743.[14] It is not unlikely that Noel himself or one, if not both of his parents, was a *piece d'inde,* for M. Carrière owned five such slaves at the time. Subsequently, Noel Carrière became free and in 1777 married Marianne Thomas, a free Negro woman.[15] To this couple, a number of children were born, one of whom a son, named Noel after his father, would serve later as a commissioned officer in the colored militia.[16] The elder Noel, as has been seen, had entered the service of his Catholic Majesty as a second lieutenant under Governor Gálvez when Spain as France's ally declared war against Great Britain. He permitted no one to doubt that he was a black man identified with the *morenos,* for he followed his signature with *Negre libre* or its abbreviation *N/l.* Francisco Dorville, a free mulatto, also entered the service under Gálvez. His career in the *pardos* closely follows that of Carrière in the *morenos.* Both Carrière and Dorville were active later in the colored corps.

The Negro troops as well as the others had little time to rest in New Orleans where they had returned after the successful river campaign. They were next needed for the Gulf expedition, plans for which Gálvez began implementing in the fall of 1779, concentrating on Mobile. Realizing that the requested number of additional troops from Havana would not be sent in time, if at all, and fearing further reinforcement of Mobile by the English, he decided to undertake the expedition with the troops at hand. Accordingly, on January 11, 1780, having already mobilized his forces, he embarked for Mobile. Altogether his forces included some 750 men: 43 men of the Regiment of Principe of the Second Battalion of Spain, 50 of the Fixed Regiment of Havana, 141 of the Fixed Regiment of Louisiana, 14 artillerymen, 26 carabiniers, 323 white militiamen, 104 free black and mulattoes, 24 slaves, and 26 Anglo-American auxiliaries.[17] Many of these colored troops had served with Gálvez the year before. Some, like Renato, a free Negro "of good conduct," received his first promotion as noncommissioned officer in the service of the Crown when he was appointed to the position of corporal second class in the company of free Negroes the day before embarkation for Mobile.[18] Successful in the passage of the Mississippi, the fleet was buffeted in the Gulf by adverse winds and storms. Finally, Gálvez and his army were before Fort Charlotte and the enemy on February 29, 1780. On March 12 the fort fell and surrendered some three hundred men and several pieces of artillery.

After taking Mobile, the expedition returned to New Orleans where Gálvez concerned himself with plans for the reduction of Pensacola, the real objective of the Gulf campaign. Realizing that the British under General John Campbell had more than two thousand troops, had readied Fort George protecting Pensacola for a decisive battle, and could expect reinforcements, Gálvez gave his immediate attention to manpower. Personally appealing to the Captain General at Havana for additional troops, he sailed for Pensacola on February 28, 1781. Included in his forces from Cuba were two battalions of colored troops from Havana, one of 130 mulattoes and the other of 134 darker grenadiers and scouts.[19]

Meanwhile, Gálvez had ordered troops in New Orleans and Mobile to rendezvous with him on Santa Rosa Island (located in front of Pensacola) or on the mainland just east of that island. Included among the troops from Louisiana were ninety free mulattoes and blacks and seventy-five Negro slaves.[20] This was the third time that many of these troops, especially the free men from New Orleans, had served under his command. But the increasing use of slaves reflected the desperate need of Gálvez for manpower at the beginning of his Pensacola campaign. To encourage them, he proclaimed that any slave who took part in the campaign would receive his freedom and one hundred pesos if he were seriously wounded, and the same reward and the privilege of purchasing his own freedom for four hundred pesos if he were slightly wounded.[21]

Effecting his troop rendezvous by March 23, Gálvez was able to open the attack against Fort George early in April. As assaults proved too costly, and he himself had been slightly wounded in a preliminary action, siege tactics were resorted to. A battery of six twenty-four pounders was planted in front of the enemy advance redoubt which was breached on April 8, blowing up the powder magazine and killing 105 of the enemy.

Gálvez immediately moved his troops forward to a more commanding position. Fort George, then exposed to heavy enemy fire which it was unable to return, surrendered. He received 1,113 men as prisoners.

He suffered casualties of 96 dead and 123 wounded; of the latter, 7 were slaves.[22] One free Negro of the colored militia, Juan Cos, was captured by the British.

Again members of the expedition came in for commendations and honors. Gálvez was highly honored for the conquest of Pensacola. He was made a count, promoted to lieutenant general, made commander of West Florida and Louisiana, which were to be independent of New Spain, and awarded ten thousand pesos. In turn he singled out others for special consideration. Simon Calfat had the distinction of being awarded a pension by General Gálvez, who was still governor. This pension was granted for life and amounted to 240 pesos a year. Carlos Calfat, sublieutenant of the *pardos,* and Pedro Thomas, lieutenant of the *morenos,* again won medals for the honorable and brave manner in which they conducted themselves.[23]

Other deserving officers of this outfit, the *milicias de color,* received a gratification as recompense for their service and to indemnify them for almost a year's absence from their families in the service of the King. Cos, who had been captured, was purchased from the Indians to whom he had been sold by the British. Juan Bautista Serraz and Juan Bautista Metzinger were promoted to sergeants in 1781.[24] The certificate of the former is dated March 26, 1781, and qualifies as a promotion in the field, as Gálvez had just begun operations against Fort George at that time.

One slave, Santiago, received a citation for bravery from General Gálvez. It took the form of an official document designed to furnish incontrovertible evidence upon all occasions of the highest quality of service rendered by the slave in the siege and conquest of Pensacola. Santiago, it specified, "has complied with his obligations with great zeal and punctuality, manifesting in the expeditions, attacks, and the defense, a decided interest in the royal service." [25] The certificate, issued in New Orleans on July 1, 1781, was signed by Gálvez in rubric.

The organization and use of the colored militia by Gálvez in the American Revolution was another step in the development of Negro soldiers in Louisiana. Not only had these troops performed creditably against the British, their first experience against trained European soldiers, but they had been commended by Gálvez for their able conduct. Moreover, they had contributed to America's winning of independence by helping to close the gateways to the American West and South through which the British planned to strike at the western flanks of the American colonies. In so doing they engaged British troops which might have been used elsewhere.[26] Whether or not the troops were aware of the urgency of their mission is unknown. Of more immediate importance to them was the fact that the war was over and they were again at home.

During peacetime, the colored militiamen also contributed to the security and welfare of the province. Their largest efforts were in pursuing and capturing runaway slaves and destroying hideouts. Shortly after their arrival home from the recent war, they were called upon for such service.

Cimarróns, as these runaway slaves were called, escaped deep into the swamps where in some inaccessible and remote place they would build a hideaway and headquarters. They then organized themselves into bands which raided plantations for weapons and food and committed crimes ranging from robbery to murder.

As these groups increased in number, they became more formidable. Sometimes they were referred to as savage Negroes. But savage or not, their life was attractive to many slaves and the *Cabildo* (the New Orleans town council) felt called upon to set up a *"cimarrón* fund" to reimburse the masters of runaway slaves killed by pursuing officers. The fund was soon exhausted, and the slaves continued to seek the wild, free life of the *cimarróns*.[27]

Raids, robberies, and repeated acts of daring were everyday occurrences. In 1782 Bautista Hagon, captain of the *pardos* of the colored militia, spent two days with a detachment of men searching in vain for *cimarróns*.[28] Four of the outlaws posing with their chief as allies to the Negro militia guided the detachment into an ambush. One of the militiamen was killed, and several were wounded. On another occasion the *cimarróns* seized Don Carlos de Villiers, lieutenant of the Company of the First Battalion. In fact, these groups became so bold that they set up companies in different places. Such was Gaillare Village, from which, under the leadership of Juan Malo, Second Knight of the Ax, continuous crimes were perpetrated.

Not only did free people of color outside of the limits of New Orleans fear for their lives but even the slaves were frightened. Many plantations outside the city were abandoned. Masters were circumspect in scolding their slaves for fear they would carry out the threat to *"cimarrón."* Moreover, there was always the possibility of the *cimarróns'* combining with other discontented slaves to form a dreaded insurrection. The *cimarróns* grew in number and became so bold that the Cabildo decided to send Lieutenant Colonel Francisco Bouligny, acting commandant of the province, against them with an adequate force composed of regulars and the white and colored militia.

This expedition, undertaken in 1784, was only partially successful, and then only after enduring unprecedented hardships. In some places the soldiers were forced to wade through water and chest-high reeds which defied the use of small canoes. In others they pushed through swamps previously thought impenetrable. Finally, they reached the outlaws' headquarters. Here they were able to capture some fifty runaways including four principal leaders. Action against them was summary—the four leaders were put to death in the public square in New Orleans, two accomplices were hanged, and fifty runaways were imprisoned.[29] Of the 3,364 pesos expended for the Cimarron War of 1784, 200 went to Madame Mandeville's slave, Chacala, who led the expedition to the hiding place, and received his freedom for this deed.[30]

The participation of the Negro militia in the Cimarron War was significant because its members were definitely placed on the side of law and order, even though other members of their own race were involved as insurrectionists. Some officials had previously doubted the loyalty of colored soldiers in such a crisis, as it had been known that the *cimarróns* had threatened the still enslaved relatives of the free people of color, as well as those free Negroes who lived outside the city limits.

Members of the Negro militia rendered yet another vital service. Like other able-bodied male citizens, they assisted in repairing crevasses in the levees of the Mississippi when necessary. Although in the strict sense such service was not military, the fact that officers in charge of the work were often the same as those in charge of the colored militiamen, and the personnel responded to such calls for duty as if they were organized on a military basis indicated a strong connection to the militia.

Breaks in the levee in the spring of 1790 demanded such service. Ninety-one free men of color—forty-two *morenos*, forty-five *pardos*, and four officers—responded for crevasse work. Each group worked alternately on both number one and number two crevasses, at the rate of three and a half *reales*, about forty cents a day and meals for the men, and four and a half *reales* per day and meals for the officers. Most of each group worked for a month or more.[31]

Officers in charge of the work included Captain Noel Carrière, captain of the *morenos*, and Bautista Hagon, captain of the *pardos*. Other officers mentioned in official documents were Charles Simon and Francisco Dorville.[32] Simon, referred to as an officer, but without mention of rank or previous experience, served thirty-one days. He rounded up the colored men of each group for work on the second crevasse. This officer performed his duty under the authorization of M. de la Barre, chief constable of the province, and worked diligently both day and night. Dorville, who is also mentioned without rank, relieved Hagon for six days. With the exception of Simon, each of the other officers had served with Gálvez against the British and had been cited by him for bravery. Moreover, two of them, Carrière and Hagon, had won promotion to captaincies. Similarly, many if not all of the men who worked on the crevasse under these officers had also served under Gálvez.

The next military service of the Negro militia occurred under Don Francisco Luis Hector, Baron Carondelet, when it figured in his defense plan for the colony in the closing decade of the nineteenth century. Carondelet, who assumed the governorship of Louisiana in 1792, was charged with the responsibility of placing the province in a state of defense in order to secure it against possible attacks from the United States and France. Vital matters disputed by America and the Spanish government in Louisiana, and rapidly reaching a critical stage, included the location of the Florida boundary, free navigation of the Mississippi, and westward expansion. About the same time Louisiana was threatened by repercussions from the French Revolution which had already spread to Haiti. Not only had many Frenchmen in Louisiana expressed sympathy for the new French Republic but a number had openly addressed a petition to that government praying that France reannex Louisiana.

Turning to his mission with vigor, Carondelet strengthened existing fortifications and built new ones on the Mississippi from the Gulf to St. Louis, and at Mobile and Pensacola. By December, 1794, he had completed his task. He was particularly proud of Fort San Felipe (Fort St. Philip) below New Orleans at Plaquemines which controlled the entrance to the Mississippi from the Gulf. He fortified New Orleans with Forts San Carlos (St. Charles), Bourgogne, (Burgundy), and San Luis (St. Louis), and further secured the city with a system of redoubts joined by a sheltered road and reinforced by a strong palisade.[33]

At the same time the Governor gave consideration to military personnel. Recognizing the impossibility of depending upon either Cuba or Spain for regular troops which might be needed quickly, he decided upon the full utilization of the entire militia. His enthusiasm and admiration for the militia grew large as he strengthened it. Not only did he believe Louisiana was unconquerable but he felt that the militia was preferable to regular troops because of their dexterity in traversing the swamps and their skill in the use of muskets.

This preference was increased by economic considerations, for Carondelet reported to the Captain General at Havana that his troops would not cost in one year what the regular troops cost in one month, "even though it be increased by the cost of two companies of colored people with its staff, each company of two hundred men under arms . . . ." [34] By his calculations, the King would have a force of 4,019 men; composed of a corps of 3,379 militia, 240 cavalrymen, and 400 free men of color.

In his report of May 31, 1792, on troop arrangement Carondelet listed and showed the employment and rate of pay for the personnel of his several organizations. His account of the colored militia provided for the major staff of these men divided into two companies of *pardos* and *morenos* of two hundred men each and gave the rate of pay, the same for each organization, by month and year for each personnel classification from private through captain. Governor Carondelet ended this particular part of his report with a notation that "the colored people served during the last year with much valor" and that during peacetime "they are the ones used in pursuing runaway Negroes (slaves) and destroying their hideouts" which were built "in places too impenetrable for regular troops." [35]

He pointed out in the same report that he had not yet had time to collect his scattered troops, but he felt nevertheless, his defense plan would enable him to meet the invasion of an army of American adventurers which, according to rumor, had collected on the Ohio and only awaited high water to descend on New Orleans. Although this threatened invasion did not materialize, Carondelet continued to improve his defenses. In his statement of military strength to the Captain General at Havana for October 31, 1792, he listed the militia of free people of color divided into a company of *morenos* and a company of *pardos* "each numbering 200 excellent marksmen with four officers." [36]

Meanwhile, the Governor gave attention to increasing the number of noncommissioned officers in the Negro militia. Between September 18, 1792, and May 30, 1794, inclusive, he issued twenty-nine commissions to the personnel of this organization. [37] Most of these, two for sergeants and twenty-three for corporals, were granted on February 1, 1793, preparatory to war with France, Spain's ally in the American Revolution.

By no means was the extensive preparedness program ill-advised, for by 1793 the French Revolution threatened the monarchical governments throughout Europe and their overseas possessions. Carondelet, expecting French invasion by way of the Gulf, assigned the colored militia to Fort San Felipe at Plaquemines as reinforcements. The men were under the immediate command of Colonel Don Gilbert Maxent, who was charged with the specific duty of preventing the enemy from landing below the fort.[38] If the enemy were successful and had a superior force, the militia was to retreat by vessel to the pass of Bayou Mardi Gras which it would defend. If the enemy forced this pass, the militia would then help to defend Fort San Felipe and, if able, pursue and harass the enemy vessels. One-half of the corps of volunteers was to be sent from the lower coast of New Orleans; if it arrived in time, it was to join the Negro militia in the action against the enemy.

Carondelet was disappointed when France passed up the opportunity to attack Louisiana by the Gulf. Instead of being able to show the effectiveness of his defense as he had hoped, he could only write the Captain General that the occasion had not presented itself to test his plans at Fort San Felipe although its defense had been carefully prepared and he had sent four hundred men to Plaquemines when the province was threatened.[39]

While the Governor was improving the defense of Louisiana against the foe from without, disturbances of a hostile nature menaced the province from within. Slave insurrections, military conspiracies, plots and counterplots (both real and fancied), reflecting the French Revolution which had already spread to Santo Domingo, began to appear.

The first slave insurrection that Carondelet had to deal with originated in Pointe Coupée on the plantation of Julian Poydras, who at the time was away in the United States of America on business. It was cleverly planned. The slaves throughout the area were to set fire to the homes of their masters, then on the pretext of trying to extinguish the flames would capture arms and begin a wholesale insurrection which would spread throughout the province. The insurrection was to begin on April 15, 1795, but the leaders quarreled and the wife of one was sent to reveal the plot to the parish commandant.[40]

The leaders were promptly arrested but the enraged followers attempted to rescue them. In the conflict which followed, several slaves lost their lives and the others took flight. Carondelet speedily restored order by meting exemplary punishment to fifty-four insurrectionists who had been originally implicated in the plot.[41] The leaders were tried, found guilty, and punished by being hanged publicly along the Royal Road and other prominent places along the Mississippi from Pointe Coupée to New Orleans. Twenty-two slaves were sentenced to ten years at hard labor, and two white men who were implicated were given six years of the same punishment. These sentences were served principally in Havana. One white man and two free Negroes, the latter recently from Haiti, and a slave were banished from Louisiana.

In the trials and investigation which followed the attempted insurrection, the Governor not only discovered that it had been a year and a half in the making and was fed by propaganda from residents of France and Santo Domingo, but also that a strong rumor persisted that the Spanish settlers were courting the Negroes and storing arms in certain homes for slaves who were to use them against the French settlers.

At the same time slaves were heard singing Jacobin songs which threatened the lives of the officials of the province. In one of the more popular songs, the slaves sang of the time when they would become republicans and freedmen, promised to guillotine the "swine governor" and hang the treasurer and the auditor.[42] Moreover, some soldiers of the Fixed Regiment of New Orleans were accused of hostility to the Governor. Trusted colored officers like Captain Charles Simon and Captain Francisco Dorville and Lieutenant Pierre Bailly were named as being in collusion with the French.[43]

As a result of a very intensive inquiry conducted by the Governor, it was found that the rumor concerning the storage of muskets for the use of slaves was absolutely groundless. The house to which it led and which was searched belonged to a very loyal Spanish subject, a Pierre Marie Cabaret de Trepy, who had previously requested the Governor to search his home in order to vindicate his name and squelch the charge. The names of Simon and Dorville were also cleared, but of Pierre Bailly more will be said later.

Shortly thereafter (the summer of 1795), word leaked out that certain soldiers of the Fixed Regiment were plotting a conspiracy. Colonel Bouligny, the commanding officer, immediately began an investigation. The main witness was Charles Joseph Lange (de'Ange), member of the colored militia, who testified that while at Plaquemines with the expedition in 1793, he met a French soldier of the Fixed Regiment named Roland with whom a friendship developed.

Lange met Roland later in New Orleans near the market, was greeted as a brother, and invited to a tavern where in company with two other men they drank and conversed. Roland informed him that they were all brothers, all French, and that it was important to sustain the country and destroy the *encargos,* meaning the Spanish. After asking Lange how many of the colored militia could be depended upon, Roland stated that he himself could count on sixty soldiers.

Advised by his father-in-law, François de Lande (Francis Delande), a free man of color, and Raphael Barnabe, a free Negro and a corporal of the Negro militia, Lange volunteered his testimony to the officials who brought the soldier to trial for attempted conspiracy. Although Roland denied the charges, there were other witnesses, including Noel Trudeau, a slave who had drunk with the group in the tavern, who substantiated Lange's story. The soldier was found guilty, and was transferred from his outfit in Louisiana to another in Pensacola, where he was to suffer punishment.[44]

The case of the free Negro militiaman Pierre Bailly was different. Bailly was an out and out sympathizer with the French Revolution. At a ball given late in 1791 by a free Negro, Esteban Lelande, he was alleged to have declared that he and his companions only awaited word from Cape François and Santo Domingo to move against the officials in New Orleans.[45] He continued to express remarks against the Spanish government and left little doubt that he embraced the principles of the revolutionists. Carondelet was of the opinion that Bailly "possessed diabolical ideas of freedom and equality." After a trial, he was sent to Havana, February 24, 1794, where he was confined as a political prisoner until after the war, when he was released and returned to Louisiana.[46]

Some excuse for Bailly's aversion to the Spanish regime may be found in what appears to be injustices he had received at the local courts of justice. In 1790 when work on the crevasse was necessary, Bailly sent one of his slaves, who died on the job. When he sued to recover damages, the Cabildo rejected his claim on the grounds that the slave died of natural causes. Having accepted the slave as a substitute for the work assigned to Bailly, the court held that it was not responsible for the charges made.[47]

Bailly had also had an unhappy experience with the law during the administration of Carondelet. He had constructed an enclosed terrace on the batture in front of his house where he stored firewood. But another person had also stored wood there. Bailly took him before Carondelet, who found against Bailly and permitted the wood to remain there as the batture was held in common.[48] For the same reason, Carondelet ordered Bailly's store on a flatboat, which was apparently anchored permanently on the batture, to be demolished if not moved.

These examples of questionable loyalty on the part of a few members of the colored militia did not injure the organization in the eyes of Carondelet. He believed that as an organization the unit had remained clear of subversion and continued its use in his defense plans for the security of the province, his major objective.

On June 5, 1797, the Governor issued a military directive in case of an alarm or attack upon New Orleans. By this order parts of both the white and colored troops were to be distributed among the strategic defense points throughout the city on a complementary basis without regard to color.[49]

Fifty mulattoes commanded by their mulatto Captain Francisco Dorville were assigned to the defense of the Redoubt San Juan (St. John) along with a company of grenadiers under Captain Francisco Riano and twenty artillerists under Captain Miguel Fortier. Thirty Negroes commanded by First Lieutenant Pedro Thomas, a free Negro, and two details of troops under the command of Captain Juan Durel and Don Francisco Durel were responsible for the security of Rampart San Juan. Lieutenant Colonel Don Manuel Perez had the superior command there. Fifty men from the company of free Negroes, commanded by their captain, Noel Carrière, were assigned to Fort San Fernando (St. Ferdinand), along with troops under Captain Don Miguel Roig and Second Lieutenant Don Pablo Darcantel. Captain Don Ignatuo Chalmet De Lino was in complete charge there. Forty men of the free mulattoes commanded by their captain Charles Simon, a free mulatto, were included among the troops to defend Fort Bourgogne. These troops were under orders of Colonel Don Andres Almonester of the militia. Thirty-five men of the company of free mulattoes and their first lieutenant, together with other troops, all commanded by Captain Don Gilberto Andry of the regulars, were placed in charge of Fort San Luis.

From this troop disposition the colored militia of New Orleans mustered no less than 205 members exclusive of officers as of June 5, 1797. Of these, 80 were free *morenos* and the remainder, 125, free *pardos*.

For this particular operation, manning defense posts around the city, they were divided into three companies: one *morenos,* commanded by Captain Noel Carrière and two *pardos,* one of which was commanded by Captain Francisco Dorville and the other by Captain Charles Simon, respectively.

Other than a few promotions in the colored militia made by Manuel Gayoso de Lemos, the successor to Governor Carondelet, and the use of the corps in an expedition during the administration of the Marquis de Casa Calvo, such was the condition of the organization when Spain in 1800 ceded Louisiana back to France, which in turn sold it to the United States. De Lemos promoted, among others, Vincent Populus, who was to gain greater prominence in the colored militia later, to sergeant first class of the *fusileros.*[50]

The Marquis de Casa Calvo, governor from 1799 to 1801, soon after his arrival in New Orleans sent an expedition, which included the colored militia, to Florida to capture the adventurer, William A. Bowles. Bowles, who with Indian allies was engaged in hostile acts against the Spanish Crown, was operating in the area of Fort St. Marks on the Apalachicola River. The expedition failed to take Bowles, but it did succeed in capturing some of his companions, along with his papers and other effects.[51]

The expedition against Bowles was the last military action in which the colored militia engaged under the colors of Spain. In October, 1800, Napoleon, through the Treaty of San Ildefonso, induced Spain to retrocede Louisiana to France in return for the creation of the Kingdom of Etruria in Tuscany for the Duke of Parma, son-in-law of the King of Spain. In March, 1801, arrangements had been completed to carry out the treaty; but the French occupation of Louisiana did not take place until 1803. Napoleon had decided to revive the French colonial empire, and the acquisition of Louisiana was a first step in that direction. He wished to win the war in Haiti, however, before venturing upon the Louisiana project.

Napoleon had arranged for Citizen Pierre Clement Laussat to come to the province as prefect to prepare for the occupation. Laussat was to be followed by General Claude Perrin Victor who was to become the Captain General of Louisiana and take possession of the colony in the name of the French Republic. Secret orders drawn up for Victor and approved by Napoleon instructed him to organize the Spanish militia of Louisiana which "is said to be very suitable for war" into a national guard. This national guard was also to include "a few small bodies of Negroes and Mulattoes" which were attached to the militia and "against whom apparently no complaint had been made."[52] These instructions were not issued as Victor did not come to Louisiana. Conditions in Europe and reverses of the French army in Haiti caused Napoleon to require his services elsewhere. Laussat possibly had a copy of these orders; he certainly was aware of them.[53]

Laussat arrived in Louisiana on March 26, 1803, to assume his duties and later, although unknown to him at the time, to receive the transfer for France. His reception was not the warmest, for there existed the grave question concerning the attitude of the French Republic toward slavery in light of the pronouncements of liberty, equality, and fraternity, and the progress of the revolution in Haiti.

Casa Calvo, who along with Juan Manuel de Salcedo, governor of Louisiana from 1801-03, was commissioned to proclaim the transfer to France, arrived in New Orleans from Havana in April, 1803, to carry out his mission. Soon after arrival, the Marquis invited all militia officers to meet with him in order to sign whether they would remain in the service of the King of Spain. They also went "to exact a yes from the two companies of men of color of this city, which composed all the workmen of the city."[54] Nor were the Spanish officials above coercion, for two colored militiamen complained to Laussat that they "were kept twenty-four hours in prison" in order to make them consent.[55]

It is doubtful that many of the militia personnel elected to remain loyal to Spain. For one thing, it was difficult for many of the inhabitants to forget that Casa Calvo had accompanied O'Reilly to the province in 1769 when the latter used drastic measures to put down the revolution of the French against the new Spanish government, that he was allied to the O'Reilly family by marriage, and that recently in 1793, he had stood by with his troops at Fort Dauphin, Santo Domingo, without raising a hand when many Frenchmen were massacred by the black revolutionists.[56] Many of the Louisianians decided to remain neutral for the time being. Very few if any of the Negroes signed under the Spanish, especially after coercion was attempted.

Laussat officially proclaimed the possession of Louisiana for France on November 30, 1803, on the same day issuing a number of decrees. Included among these were the appointment of Deville de Groutins Bellechasse as colonel and commander of the militia of New Orleans "including the companies of free men of color" and the recommissioning of all officers of the militia.[57] Shortly thereafter, Laussat by special proclamation reaffirmed the Black Code.[58]

Within twenty days Louisiana would be acquired by the United States of America. With the acquisition would come an organized and disciplined colored militia which, in the service of Spain, had earned a bright military reputation for defending Louisiana from both internal and external foes. What would be the disposition of such a legacy by the United States?

CHAPTER III

STRUGGLE FOR AMERICAN RECOGNITION

WITHIN A WEEK after receiving the formal transfer of Louisiana, William C. C. Claiborne, whom President Jefferson appointed provisional governor, informed Washington of his problem with the colored militia and sought advice concerning its status. Although it was only one of the many problems confronting Claiborne incident to assimilating a people well established in a Latin culture into a nation rooted in the Anglo-Saxon tradition, to him it was his principal difficulty and seemed insurmountable.[1]

Upon this corps—two large companies—he had "reflected with much anxiety" only to be faced with a most difficult dilemma. "To recommission them, on the one hand would be considered an outrage" by certain parts of the Union, especially the South, where such status was prohibited by established policy. On the other hand, Claiborne continued, "to disband them would be to raise an armed enemy in the very heart of the country and to disarm them would savor too strongly of that desperate system of government which seldom succeeds." [2] That the companies had been officially attached to the services of Spain, who esteemed them very serviceable, then had been transferred to France, who in turn recognized them and passed them on to America, only complicated matters for Claiborne. The situation was worsened further by the fact that Spain, whose possessions bounded America's territory on the west and east, kept open her invitation to the colored militia to join her service. What, Claiborne wished to know, should be the official position on the question of recognition?

His request for guidance concerning the colored militia reflected a perplexity born of inexperience as well as a want of authority. Never in his political career, first as enrolling clerk in Congress in 1790, then judge and later congressional representative of Tennessee, and finally as governor of the Mississippi Territory just prior to his new appointment, had he been confronted with this kind of problem. Nor was this surprising, for a body of armed Negro militiamen in muster during peacetime was entirely out of place in the South if not elsewhere in the United States. But Claiborne's experience in Mississippi where, before coming to New Orleans, he had dealt with slaves, Indians, and Spanish subjects as well as white Americans made him too astute a politician to ignore the status of the colored militia in New Orleans and that of the free people of color from which it was drawn.

The free people of color represented about one fourth of the free population of New Orleans and vicinity at this time, a proportion all the more significant because the diversity of groups in the little international outpost made the city a combination of minorities. There were the French and Spanish and their descendants born in the colony, known as Creoles, as well as Italians, Portuguese, Germans, Acadians, Americans, and Negroes, including both slaves and free. The total population, some eight thousand at the time of the transfer in 1803, was approximately equally divided between whites and nonwhites. Most of the free people of color lived in the city where they were an important segment of the skilled working group. Some operated small businesses and owned considerable property. Others resided in the country where they cultivated cotton and other products on their small tracts.

Benjamin Morgan, a prominent settler from the states who was active in both business and politics, was impressed by this group. Writing to Chandler Price, his influential political friend in Washington, he wanted to know "upon what footing will the free quadroon, mulatto, and black people stand. Will they be entitled to the rights of citizens or not." [3] Observing that they were a numerous class in the city, and that many members were very respectable, he pointed out that under the Spanish government they enjoyed "rights in common with other subjects" [4] and could certainly become an asset to a new country. Morgan believed it was "worth the consideration of the government that they may be made citizens" instead of "formidable abettors of slaves." [5] Morgan's comments, included in his letter to Price on conditions in New Orleans and the need of care in the selection of public officials for Louisiana, revealed more than a firsthand impression concerning the people of color. They reflected an insight into the important problem of adjustment.

How would they adjust? They were a closely knit, proud class of people many of whose members could trace their ancestry through two and three generations of freedom. They were never forgetful of the fact that they had come under the jurisdiction of the young American Republic as free men, nor were they unmindful of their Creole heritage. They were especially proud of their militia whose roots were planted deep in the past of Louisiana, whose record had been commendable, and to which every able-bodied man of their group belonged. At the time of the American acquisition, their militia was among the few (if not the only) outfits most completely organized. Moreover, it had just taken part in the ceremonies of the transfer.[6]

Membership in the Negro militia also carried a social significance in the colored community inasmuch as many of its members were leaders in other areas. Ranking officer personnel enjoyed additional prestige by their position and were in demand at weddings, baptisms, and the like where they signed their names by rank and title, giving such affairs an additional status symbol. The wedding of a fellow officer or one of their children like Felicite Brulé, daughter of Charles Brulé, free mulatto captain in the colored militia, at St. Louis Cathedral on March 19, 1804, was a special event being both a military wedding and a nuptial mass.[7]

In light of such considerations, Claiborne decided for the time being to await orders from the State Department unless necessity compelled action. But he left no doubt that the matter was urgent. He ended his communication with the hope of receiving these directions as soon as possible.

Before instructions from Washington arrived, the colored militia took matters into their own hands. They presented an address from their organization to Claiborne offering its service to the new Governor.[8] Fifty-five members signed the memorial. Prominent among these were Louis Simon, who signed first; Charles Simon, who had been a captain under Carondelet; and others like Baltazare Demozeillier, Philippe August, Baptiste Hardy, Maurice Populus, Louis Liotant, and Charles Porée, who had attained or would attain prominence in the colored militia mainly as officer personnel.[9]

Referring to themselves in the memorial as free citizens of Louisiana, the men professed sincere attachment to the United States. Such virtues of the new Republic as personal and political freedom, justice and liberality of which they now felt assured, especially impressed them. They next related their military service under Spain explaining how their conduct was of the highest, and promised that if so "honored by the American Government," they would serve "with fidelity and zeal." Then came the tender of service. "We therefore respectfully offer our services to the Government as a corps of volunteers agreeable to any arrangement which may be thought expedient." [10] The petition was ended with a congratulatory statement to the new governor.

Claiborne quickly sensed the significance of the memorial and the influence its signers carried in the Negro community. After giving it the necessary study, he forwarded it under date of January 17, 1804, to Secretary of State James Madison.

It was a skillfully drawn document, not without psychological overtones concerning status, yet devoid of any assertion designed to provoke animosity. While tendering service and expressing praise over what had happened, the men through their document conveyed to the officials of the federal government the belief that their personal and political freedom would be respected and that they would be treated with justice and liberality.

Their hopes for equality under the new government were expressed in the document. They contended that this equality was supported not only by the great truths upon which the United States had been founded but also by Article III of the treaty of acquisition. This latter provided that the inhabitants of the territory would be admitted as soon as possible to the United States, according to the principles of the federal Constitution and would be permitted to enjoy all the rights, advantages, and immunities of the citizens of that country.[11]

In other words, the militiamen, through their memorial, sought to gain the fullest measure of citizenship under the new government and used their military record in the past and its promise for the future as a gilt-edged justification. Their gesture was most timely. It placed them on record at the very outset, almost before the ink on the treaty dried, as seekers of full freedom in the United States of America, a country dedicated to the democratic principles, and whose freedom they had helped to win albeit under the flag of an ally. Whether intended or not, they thus put to an early test the dedication of the federal government and the American people to the principles upon which the country was founded. They were the first organized group of Negroes to do so in such a manner.

But there was another side to the memorial. The status of the militia of free men of color of Louisiana had to be considered in an entirely new context. Louisiana was now an integral part of the young Republic and no longer a minor outpost in the imperial scheme of the old world powers. True, freedom and equality were springboards of the "American Dream." But the dream was just unfolding and must from the beginning face the harsh reality of capitalistic slavery.

Whatever the outcome, the free men of color had shown that they were not indifferent to their freedom and responsibility under the new government. They had made a strong bid for recognition; attaining it would not be easy. There would first have to be territorial then state accommodation.

It is not likely that the free people of color knew at the outset that Governor Claiborne regarded their militia as a problem and had sought advice from Washington as to its disposition. They may or may not have been aware of the fact that Claiborne in September, 1803, fearing a demonstration from the free colored population, had requested President Jefferson to ship ammunition and four or five thousand stands of arms.[12] And on the day following the transfer of the province, General James Wilkinson, commander of the American army (who along with Claiborne had received Louisiana for America), requested secretary of war Henry Dearborn to insure the peace by assigning to New Orleans five hundred regulars as he found "the formidable aspect of the armed Blacks and mulattoes officered and organized painful and perplexing."[13]

By January 11, 1804, General Wilkinson had changed his opinion considerably. At that time he still urged the secretary of war to send more troops for a strong garrison, because the Spanish not only had more troops in the city than the American government but the inhabitants were ridiculing America's puny forces with "what a sad government."[14] He felt that the jealousies of the people of color and the whites appeared to be increasing, but if he could judge from what he heard and saw, the former "are most to be relied upon by us."[15]

The Negroes of New Orleans had universally mounted the eagle in their hats and avowed their attachment to the United States, while the whites of the city still demonstrated their love for their mother country and revealed the fond hope that some incident of the European war might restore them to her. Wilkinson cautioned Dearborn that he spoke generally. He added, however, that because all the people of color were armed, he felt that a bold incendiary, by playing upon their fears and raising their hopes, might produce the horrible scenes of bloodshed and rapine occurring in Santo Domingo. Governor Claiborne, as events proved, became their protagonist.

Claiborne's verbal reply to the memorial was apparently made immediately after having received the address which was possibly read and then presented to him for record. He informed the Negroes that "under the protection of the United States, their liberty, property, and religion were safe" and that "their confidence in the American Government would increase as they became acquainted with the principles, wisdom, and virtue with which it was administered." [16]

As to the tender of military service, Claiborne pointed out that he would not attempt a general reorganization of the militia until he had received particular instructions from the President, but in the meantime "they would remain in the same situation in which the former government had placed them." [17] He concluded by assuring them of his confidence in their military zeal and in the sincerity of their professions of loyalty to the United States.

Claiborne's statement lacked nothing in diplomacy. It neither made rash promises nor did it estrange the colored militiamen. Favorable impressions of each for the other and respect, if not mutual trust, could not but help come from this exchange.

On February 20, 1804, about a month after the presentation of the address, Secretary Dearborn replied to Claiborne concerning the colored militia. After having given "this subject of some delicacy" serious consideration, he advised Claiborne either to continue the organization as it had been set up by the Spaniards or to renew it.[18] He was to follow whichever alternative seemed more expedient. At the same time, he was advised not to increase the strength of the corps but if possible to diminish it, if this could be done without offending the Negro personnel. Furthermore, in the selection and appointment of the principal officers, respectability and integrity of character, as well as popularity and influence among associates were to be the governing factors.

Finally, as a token of trust which the United States government placed in the colored militia, the Secretary suggested the appropriateness of presenting the outfit with a small, inexpensive flag or standard which would be satisfactory to the corps. If a silk one were deemed necessary, he felt it could be painted in New Orleans; otherwise, it might be bunting like the flags for sea service. In the same letter, he informed Claiborne that his organization of the other militia companies met the President's fullest approbation.

Claiborne was in full accord with Dearborn on the point of recognition of the colored militia. He felt it was the wisest course to pursue under the existing circumstances. Meanwhile, he busied himself with implementing plans concerning the entire militia. On April 30, the first anniversary on which the Treaty of France was signed for the purchase of Louisiana, he presented to the Battalion of Orleans Volunteers, an organization of white soldiers, a beautiful standard which was received with great enthusiasm.

A banner for the regiment of city militia and one for the battalion of free people of color were to be presented later. The color standard for the militia regiment like that for the volunteers was obtained from General Wilkinson to avoid additional expense. Both had been little used and were formerly attached to the Fourth Regiment. The ensign for the Negroes, a new one, was made in the city. By presenting each outfit with a standard, Claiborne felt he would prevent dissension between white and colored militia.

In June, 1804, the governor appointed as senior major and commander of the Negro unit, Michel Fortier, a wealthy merchant and native of New Orleans. The position of junior major went to Lewis Kerr, a relative of Claiborne and former resident of Mississippi but more recently of New Orleans. Both officers were white. These appointments were not entirely satisfactory to the personnel of the battalion, for they were desirous of being commanded by men of their own color as they had been in the past and they were particularly averse to Fortier. However, after a conference between the governor, company officers, and several of the most influential men of the militia, the appointments were concurred in.[19]

Meanwhile, a muster of the former members of the colored militia was undertaken. New recruits were not to be enrolled and mustering officers were instructed to disclaim any knowledge of why such a decision had been made.[20]

On June 21, 1804, the Governor presented a stand of colors to the battalion. It was made of white silk ornamented with fifteen alternating red and white stripes. The standard, according to Claiborne, was gratefully received and elicited expressions of responsibility and gratitude.[21]

In his communication to the Secretary of War, Governor Claiborne failed to mention that a guard had been posted around the square to control the mob, if necessary, when the colored militia paraded.[22] Although nothing happened to mar the occasion, discord between the whites of Louisiana and the black militiamen began to grow. Even many of the oldest inhabitants preferred to see the organization neglected and disbanded, if its continuance would lead to discord.

The Governor admitted he was unable to determine the cause of the trouble with accuracy, but the fact of its existence was unquestionable. On the other hand, he felt the more thoughtful part of society favored his policy. Because of such feelings, he was convinced that the battalion should be managed with delicacy and caution. The complaint of a leading citizen that he was struck by the musket of a sentinel of the colored organization for interrupting him while on duty did not help the cause of the Negro military. He observed that this was the first time to his knowledge that a complaint had been lodged against the group.[23] It by no means would be the last.

Meanwhile, a number of white citizens met at the call of Edward Livingston, a celebrated former New York politician who had recently moved to New Orleans (where he would become an eminent lawyer), for the purpose of drafting a petition to Congress requesting that three grievances be corrected. First, they demanded the immediate admission of Louisiana into the United States as promised allegedly in the treaty; second, they demanded that the slave trade, which Claiborne had closed by virtue of territorial law stemming from the Ordinance of 1787, be reopened; and third, they opposed the division of Louisiana into Orleans Territory and Louisiana Territory.

The Negro population was dissatisfied, if not indignant, at not receiving an invitation to the meeting of citizens who memorialized Congress and decided to have their own meeting. Accordingly, a message was prepared inviting the free men of color to meet to discuss their rights and the propriety of drafting a memorial to Congress. This document was given to a printer for publication, who declined to print it after he had digested the contents so that he could repeat them to the Governor.[24] Claiborne, in a communication to the Secretary of State, expressed the belief that the free Negroes were well attached to the American government and that consultation with them would take care of the situation. He added, however, he would use other means if necessary.

The Governor met with nine of the more influential leaders of the free people of color and in the presence of the mayor expressed his disapproval of their letter and the contemplated meeting. Confronted with official disapproval, they not only agreed to abandon the project, but also gave the most unqualified assurance of their peaceful disposition and devoted attachment to the present government and good order.[25]

The Governor did not attempt to discover and punish the author of the letter as many wished him to do, for he felt the indignation of the whites was so great as to do the writer of the memorial bodily harm.[26] This, Claiborne advised, could furnish precisely the background for an affair in Louisiana similar to that of Santo Domingo where an original dispute between whites and mulattoes had set off a bitter struggle which eventually involved all racial groups. After considering the whole matter, Claiborne concluded that the independent action by the colored population had so aroused the animosity of the whites that any meeting held would be poorly attended.

But the status of the battalion was not yet fixed. Despite the favorable attitude of Governor Claiborne, it was continuously opposed as a body by many of the inhabitants of New Orleans. The opposition became so powerful that the unit was inactivated by omission from the militia law in October 1, 1804, when the first territorial government was established. Six months later, on April 10, 1805, the Legislative Council of the Territory of Orleans again omitted the battalion.[27]

There was no doubt that the criticism directed against Governor Claiborne and the Negro militia which appeared in the Louisiana *Gazette* on January 29, 1805, was shared by a large portion of the community. This criticism appeared in the newspaper in a letter signed "a Louisianan" and took issue with the Governor for his haste in organizing the colored corps, for presenting them with a standard similar to that of the white militia, and for "putting up with their disrespectful refusal of the officers whom he had appointed as their adjutants." [28] It was observed, in addition, that the ensign presented to the colored militia was too large and that the black captains would outrank the white adjutants who would have the rank of lieutenant.

The adverse criticism, as well as this action on the part of the government of Orleans Territory, was disappointing to the free people of color. Official neglect embittered them considerably against the American government, and it became questionable how far their loyalty to America would extend in case of real danger. Their dissatisfaction, according to Stephen, a free Negro, led them to plot against the Americans.[29]

Testifying under oath before Governor Claiborne on January 23, 1806, Stephen claimed that every free Negro man, with a few exceptions, met nightly to discuss plans detrimental to the government. When pressed for information on the place of meeting, Stephen stated that there was no one place where the group met, that on occasion they might be found at Chavare's opposite La Nuces, at the residence of Francisco Dorville—the mulatto captain who flaunted a Spanish cockade—opposite Moralle's, at Becke's near the Bayou St. John, and at other places. They all had guns with powder and balls and other military arms.

The Spanish were alleged to be involved, for a sympathizer circulated a paper, obviously for signatures, in order to ascertain those who were friendly to the Spanish. According to Stephen, they waited only the return of the Marquis Casa Calvo to give the signal to commence an attack and to free all slaves who would join them. Calvo, it was said, was expected at any time with some three or four thousand troops, as well as Indian allies. The word "fire" appeared to have been the signal, for the informer warned Americans if they heard that word, not to go out but to stand their guard. Other names which occurred in the testimony included: "Medsinger, (A Spanish officer), and Charles Brulé, a yellow man called Captain of the Grandies." [30]

Claiborne did not accept the testimony of Stephen in its entirety; yet he did not totally discredit it. For it was claimed the Spanish not only had encouraged slaves to escape to Spanish territory where they were given asylum, but they had also "tampered" with the free colored population.[31]

It is beyond question that some Negroes were devoted to the Spanish cause and that some of the officers of the colored militia felt keenly the loss of their commissions. Francisco Dorville, for instance, who had appended to his signature on notarized records at St. Louis Cathedral the term *"commandante de mulatos"* (commander of the mulattoes), now added the qualifying *"que en Tiempo de la Dominación Española"* (during the time of the Spanish domination).[32] As a precautionary measure, the Governor ordered a militia company on guard every night.

At the same time, many of the whites felt that the free people of color, having been stripped of their arms, were in no position to cause trouble. Moreover, there were several among the leaders of the free Negroes who owned considerable property and enjoyed a good reputation in the community. It was considered unlikely that such stable members of the group would become involved in any uprising. With these factors in mind, Governor Claiborne felt that proper exertion should be made to conciliate the good will of all. Despite this, however, the battalion was omitted again from the militia act of May, 1806.

In his annual speech before the two houses in joint session in January, 1807, Claiborne gave special notice to this continuing problem. After mentioning the war abroad, peace and prosperity at home, and paying a tribute to George Washington, he passed to local subjects which he felt required early attention and legislation. Among these he included the revision of the judiciary system, the necessity of a census report, an efficient control of receipts and expenditures, revision and enforcement of the civil code, and the strengthening of the militia law.

He then referred to the colored militiamen suggesting the advisability of recognizing the free men of color in New Orleans as part of the regular militia. He pointed out that under the government of Spain they formed a separate battalion which was very useful, and explained that he had continued them on the same footing. Then he added a slight compliment: "It is but justice to say, that their conduct was such as to convince me that the measure was a proper one." [33] Reminding the legislature that the corps had been neglected and omitted from the militia bill, he pointedly remarked "that the officers who were attached to it, and it is believed the privates are still desirous to compose a Separate Militia Corps." [34]

Governor Claiborne must have anticipated some success from his reference to the Negro militia in his speech. Four days earlier he had directed Colonel Henry Hopkins, adjutant general of the Territory militia, to ascertain the number of free men of color then residing in New Orleans and its vicinity who formerly were members of the colored organization. Names of officers, both commissioned and noncommissioned, were to be compiled for their immediate organization "*in the event the Legislature should by Law declare them a permanent Militia Corps* [sic]." [35]

Perhaps he was encouraged by a letter of January 26, 1807, from the House of Representatives of the Louisiana Territory which informed him that it would give the battalion of free men of color the activity it desired. But the action of the legislature did not extend beyond words. Nevertheless, Claiborne still expressed faith in the organization and continued to seek favorable legislation for it. In fact, his interest in the outfit as well as his honesty and integrity led him into an extensive controversy with one of his critics, Daniel Clark, formerly American consul at New Orleans and later territorial delegate to Congress, which finally culminated in a duel.

On May 23, 1807, the *Louisiana Gazette* of New Orleans reported extracts allegedly from a speech made by Daniel Clark, in Congress on

December 24, 1806, which indicated that a military corps under his command was organized to defend Louisiana if necessary at the transfer in 1803, that the militia had since been neglected and was totally unorganized. He charged that a black corps had been preferred to it and a standard publicly given it, while the white troops' repeated offers and wishes to be employed in their country's service were rejected. The article ended with the statement that Louisianians would expose their lives and fortunes in the defense of the territory and would rally around the standard if the men who were appointed to the command could inspire confidence.

Governor Claiborne, learning of these statements, sent a letter and a copy of the publication by special messenger to Clark to ascertain whether the extracts contained true statements of what he had reputedly said. On the following day Clark replied, acknowledging the statements. However, the report of Clark's speech to Congress as it occurred in the congressional *Annals* was not the same as the extracts of the *Gazette*.[36]

According to the congressional account, Clark said that the people of the Territory had offered their services to the United States, but that the Governor had given preference to another corps. He did not specifically name the colored corps but the reference was not mistaken in Louisiana, although it may have been in Congress.

Clark's remarks followed those of other congressmen who were debating defense of the frontier in consideration of measures to be taken in light of President Jefferson's reference to this matter in his recent message to Congress. Claiborne sent another communication to Clark in which he denied these charges of neglect of the militia and offered substantial proof in the form of a testimony by Colonel Henry Hopkins. Claiborne was especially incensed at Clark's charges pertaining to the Negro troops, and he left the congressman no doubt about his feelings.

The Governor admitted that during the temporary government of Louisiana he had organized the free men of color into a separate battalion and had given them a standard. This was done, he added, with the knowledge and approbation of the Secretary of War, but he pointed out that nothing was intended to cause dissatisfaction to any other corps. Since October, 1804, however, the battalion had ceased to exist. As a parting shot, Claiborne made clear his position regarding the colored corps. Although he had doubts as to the expediency of recognizing this group in the beginning, "yet I must confess I do not approve of the policy which refused to continue it." [37] To this explanation Clark replied with emphasis that his charge of the general neglect of the militia of the Territory he would never retract.

Claiborne informed Clark that this was only one of the complaints and that the remarks concerning the unorganized state of the troops and the black corps being "preferred while their own repeated offers to be employed in their country's service had been neglected" went much further than a general accusation of neglect.[38]

When Clark continued in his refusal either to explain further his alleged statements or retract them, Claiborne demanded satisfaction. Clark accepted the challenge, and in the subsequent duel, by pistol, Claiborne was wounded.[39] Clark escaped injury. The entire account of the affair, including copies of the correspondence preceding it, was forwarded to President Jefferson by Claiborne who, although a bit apologetic for his conduct, felt he was justified because public confidence in him and his administration was involved.

The battalion of free men of color did not benefit directly from this turn of events except to be reassured of the esteem in which the Governor held them, which had already been shown through his sense of justice and fairness, along with political expediency. Indeed, it might have injured the cause, for so much was said against that organization in 1809 that the Legislative Council decided to omit notice of the mulatto corps in the general militia law.

Reasons for the failure of the legislature to recognize the colored militia were many and varied. Petty jealousy of Claiborne and whimsical prejudices against the free people of color played a part, but although little publicized, there was a basic and genuine feeling of insecurity engendered by the thought that, when combined, the non-white population of slave and free people of color in New Orleans always exceeded the white population. According to the census prepared by Daniel Clark for President Jefferson in 1803, there were 8,080 people in the city at that time. Of these 1,355 were free people of color, 2,777 were slaves, and 3,948 were white, including 700 not domiciled.[40]

Although this return was inaccurate (Clark himself admitted the omission of the free people of color in the second quarter of the city), it showed a slight excess of nonwhites over whites. Seamen and soldiers of garrisons, however, who were not included, might have balanced the ratio. The census of 1805 by Matthew Flannery, which was far more accurate, showed a total of 8,475 persons. Of this number, 3,551 were white, 1,566 were free people of color, 3,105 were slaves, and 253 were included under all other persons.[41] The proportion was, 4,671 non-whites to 3,804 whites, including 253 in the unclassified category.

Nor did the record of the free people of color for law and order erase the fears of the white population. In addition, groupings of the French, Spanish, and Americans, exclusive of the color problem, tended to create unrest in the small settlement. However, as time passed, the white element tended to forget their differences in the face of what they considered the danger of united action from the alliance of slave and free groups.

This situation, ominous within itself, was accentuated by the increase in immigration from the French West Indies and Cuba as an outgrowth of the Haitian revolution and this brought threatened danger nearer. Early in 1804 John Watkins (Claiborne's private agent), reported twelve Negroes, allegedly brigands from Santo Domingo, who came ashore as they passed up the Mississippi near New Orleans and frightened the inhabitants with tales of horror in Santo Domingo.[42] As a result, General Wilkinson was authorized to issue orders to hold all vessels with slaves until they were cleared for passage. Such an inspection service did little good, for in July of 1804 Claiborne admitted that no effectual way had been found to prevent the entrance of West Indian Negroes into the colony.

Not until 1806, when the first legislature of the Territory passed an act to prevent the introduction of free people of color from Hispaniola and the French islands to America, was any definite control effective. This law, however, permitted colored women and children under fifteen years of age to enter, as it was felt that they fled the island from fear.[43] In the following year an act was passed prohibiting the entrance of all free Negroes into the territory. Infractions carried a penalty of twenty dollars for each week a free Negro man remained in Louisiana illegally. If the penalty were not paid, the person could be sold by the parish judge for a price equaling the fine.[44]

In 1809 these laws practically broke down under the influx of immigrants. In that year Napoleon invaded Spain, forced the royal family to abdicate, and assumed control of the government. Hostilities soon spread to the Spanish colonies. Cuba, where many French people with their slaves, and many loyalist free people of color had fled the revolution of Santo Domingo, now became hostile. In April of that year, a proclamation was issued peremptorily ordering them to leave the island or suffer possible loss of life and property. American ships in port were requisitioned to transport them to America.

Between May 10 and August 19, 1809, fifty ships landed at New Orleans from various Cuban ports with 6,060 immigrants. Of these, 1,887 were white, 2,060 free people of color, and 2,113 slaves.[45] Governor Claiborne felt he could not turn these unfortunate and impoverished people away, although he admitted he would have preferred to see Americans settle in their stead in New Orleans. Moreover, Maurice Rogers, the United States consul at Santiago, Cuba, had requested Claiborne to extend every consideration to these refugees.[46]

Confronted with this situation, Claiborne kept himself informed on the émigrés. In the report made to him by Mayor James Mather on July 18, he learned that the "Blacks" were strictly disciplined and were either Africans recently brought into Cuba or faithful slaves who had fled with their masters from Santo Domingo as early as 1803. As for the free people of color, Mather observed that he had not heard one single complaint against their conduct since their arrival. Most of them had some skill and some possessed property. He reported, however, that he had required the posting of a bond from those considered dangerous as a guarantee that they would leave the Territory within a given time.[47] The whites were said to be former planters and merchants of Santo Domingo who had gone to Cuba years previously and were presented as being both active and industrious.

In his report to Claiborne in August, Mather pointed out that he had caused all free colored male émigrés over fifteen to give security for their departure from the territory. However, only 64 out of a possible 262 known entrants had subscribed to bonds of this effect. Many whose appearance was required by the commissary of police and who were granted delay in proving their freedom or providing securities had since disappeared.[48] As far as the Mayor knew, only a few had left Louisiana. In a report for March, 1810, the Mayor noted that he had issued passports for twenty-nine men of color who were leaving for St. Bartholomew because they could not earn a livelihood in the Territory.[49] There is no doubt that most of the free colored émigrés remained in and around New Orleans.

Meanwhile, in an attempt to discourage further immigration the Governor wrote to Consul Rogers to advise prospective émigrés of the overcrowded conditions in New Orleans and to encourage them to seek asylum in some other part of the United States. As to the free people of color, he urged the Consul to discourage them from emigrating to the Territory of Orleans. "We have already a much greater proportion of that population than comports with the general interests." [50] Rogers was specifically requested to make known to them that the women and children had been received, but the male population above the age of fifteen, in pursuance to Law, had been ordered to depart. Similar information was also communicated to consuls or other agents of the United States at Guadeloupe, Martinique, and other adjacent islands.[51]

Such efforts on the part of the Governor did little good in halting the flow of Cuban émigrés to Louisiana, because the federal government shortly came to their aid. In the latter part of 1809 Congress passed an act for the remission of certain penalties for forfeitures and other purposes which had resulted by the introduction of slaves into the country. According to the Secretary of State, who carried out the measure, this was to apply in Louisiana to the migrants from Cuba and their slaves only.[52] Émigrés with their slaves from other foreign countries were subject to the general law prohibiting the introduction of slaves.

It would indeed be hazardous to attempt the exact figure by which the population of the Territory of Orleans was increased by the influx from Cuba. There is no doubt, however, that much of the growth of the population by 1810, as compared with that of 1805, was due to this movement. In 1810 the population of New Orleans was 12,225, of which 4,507 were white, 3,332 free people of color, and 4,386 slaves.[53] The number of nonwhite people combined was 7,718. For Orleans Territory the ratio was even more disproportionate. The total population was 24,552. But of this number 8,001 were white and the rest, 5,727 free people of color and 10,824 slaves.[54] In the minds of some white people of Louisiana, a slave insurrection led, directed, or in any way aided by free men of color trained in the use of arms was not beyond the realm of possibility, especially since some of the Negro former militiamen were disgruntled over the failure of the territorial legislature to recognize their organization.

In fact, the ever-present rumor and threat of slave revolts became a reality in 1811. At that time an insurrection broke out on the plantation of Colonel Manuel Andry, about forty miles above the city on the left bank of the river. After wounding the colonel and murdering his son, some several hundred slaves and their leaders forced other slaves to join them as they descended rapidly on the city, leaving in their wake destruction of life and property.[55]

According to General Wade Hampton, who arrived in New Orleans just prior to the outbreak and whom Governor Claiborne sent against the slaves, "the confusion was great beyond description." [56] The regular force in the city was inconsiderable—and there was nothing like an

organized militia. As soon as two companies of volunteer militia could
be formed, Hampton joined them to thirty regular troops and marched
out to meet the foe. Enroute they overtook a company of seamen on the
march who joined them.

At Colonel Michel Fortier's sugar works, about eighteen miles from
the city, they met the slave insurrectionists who retreated in silence as
the line advanced. After being forced back, the Negroes were attacked
by a group of young men from the other side of the river, who injured
many and dispersed others. The troops led by General Hampton then
moved in to the attack. Meanwhile, Major Homer Milton with one detachment of light infantry and another of dragoons came from Baton
Rouge to aid them. Sixty-six slaves were killed in the encounter or were
hanged soon after capture, and a number were taken to New Orleans
for trial.[57]

In his message to the officials conducting the trials, Claiborne urged
that not only justice but also mercy be shown whenever possible. He
pardoned one slave, Theodore, belonging to Archilles Truard, after he
had been tried, convicted, and sentenced to death. Theodore had made
full confession to three leading men of the community just prior to his
capture for which his freedom had been promised. Furthermore, his
master testified concerning his former good conduct. These were sufficient grounds for the Governor.[58] Again bodies were displayed along
the road from the scene of the start of the insurrection to the city as a
reminder of the penalty for uprisings.

During the insurrection New Orleans was obviously in great danger.
The general assembly was adjourned for two weeks and the city placed
under what amounted to martial law. As a security measure, the Governor placed the whole militia under arms.

The free men of color, according to Claiborne, manifested the greatest zeal for the public safety at this time. They offered their services during the crisis; one company was accepted, and was placed under the command of Major Peter F. Dubourg, a prominent citizen. According to
the Governor, this outfit performed its tour of duty "with great exacti-
tude and propriety." [59]

More than any single event, Claiborne felt that the uprising would
drive home the necessity of a strong militia for the protection of the
Territory. He informed Colonel Andry and Major Antoine St. Amand,
who had been under fire in the disturbance, that he would not permit
the next legislature to adjourn without strongly urging such a measure.[60]

Consequently, on January 29, 1811, the Governor pressed for the enactment of a strong militia law in his address to the territorial legislature.[61] Both bodies, the Legislative Council and the house of representatives, agreed to the general reasoning of the executive and promised to give the organization of an adequate militia proper consideration. Nothing of moment was done at the time, but on February 5, 1811, the legislature passed a resolution urging that any slave who distinguished himself in the late insurrection by saving his master's life or the life of any white person should be reported to the governor, and by him to the legislature within fifteen days for action.[62]

It is not clear how many slaves Claiborne recommended for consideration on February 25, but it is certain that he used the occasion to present to the legislature, among other matters for consideration, "an instrument of writing" signed by several respectable inhabitants bearing testimony "to the good conduct of certain free men of color during the late insurrection" and "recommending them [to] the favorable attention of the Legislature." [63] Although nothing was done immediately, Claiborne's persistence was not without reward, for events of international, national, and local significance in crescendo movement now came to his aid.

Louisiana was admitted to the United States, April 8, 1812. On June 12, 1812, the United States declared war on Great Britain. By this time Claiborne was casting envious eyes at Pensacola and Mobile—Spanish territory he had considered essential to the protection of Louisiana. Perhaps the Spanish learned of his ideas, for about July 20, some five weeks after the declaration of war, a new Spanish governor with about 150 Negro troops appeared in Pensacola.[64] On the same day a committee of three, Abner Duncan, Stephen Hopkins, and John Duhamel, was appointed to answer the Governor's address.

Furthermore, on July 31 committeeman Duhamel carried a resolution in the house that a committee of five be appointed to study the militia organization. The resolution was approved and Duhamel himself was named chairman, to report within eight days on progress made.[65] On August 12, the chairman presented the report of the committee to the house. Meanwhile on the same day the answer to the Governor's address was read to the house, adopted, and transmitted to the Governor.

The reply was both timely and patriotic. It commended the Governor for nurturing seeds of republican principles for nine years among inhabitants unaccustomed to the "precious boon of liberty" to the time when they entered statehood to enjoy the privileges of a wise and free people. It promised that nothing would be omitted in organizing the new government so that it could proceed with vigor. With reference to his passage concerning the war, it took high ground. Even though Louisianians were not as great in number and means as their "brethren in the north and east" they were unexcelled in their attachment to the general government. Should war approach they would repair to the standards of the country and defend them unto death.[66]

The Governor, impressed more by deeds than words, straightway sent a message to the general assembly in which he urged that body to enact with promptness such measures which the safety of the state required. Of these he singled out the militia, already disorganized and becoming worse daily, as being in immediate need of strengthening. He specifically asked that the manner of appointing ranking officers be spelled out, as there were many vacancies and no power to fill them.

Pointing out the desirability of a new militia system (as the one left by the territorial government was inefficient), he nevertheless advised at this time simply a remedy of the more permanent defects of the existing law. He felt this was expedient inasmuch as the present crisis would not permit the delay necessary for a studied reflection and mature consideration of a new bill. The legislature was requested particularly to empower the executive to carry in defense of the state "*our whole force, or such part thereof* [sic]" as the occasion may demand.[67]

Thus urged, the militia bill went through a second reading on Saturday, August 15, 1812, and was placed on the agenda as the order of business for the following Monday. On August 17, 18, 21, and 22 the house, as a committee of the whole, worked a part of each day on the bill. Its work of the twenty-second was interrupted by a message from the Governor, reinforced by a letter of August 14 from General James Wilkinson, which called upon the state to raise 2,200 volunteer troops.[68]

These troops, the General explained, were to be used to awe the Indians, secure internal tranquility, and repel foreign invasion. Regular troops of the line were to be held in readiness for any action against the enemy on land or sea. The recent declaration of war, commencement of hostilities, and the movements of the Spanish governor in Pensacola, convinced Wilkinson of the necessity of his request. This was in line with his authority from the President. Governor Claiborne's message repeated with emphasis the necessity of prompt action on the militia bill in order that he might comply with the request made of him.

The lower house resumed consideration of the militia bill on the twenty-third. On August 24 sections 7 through 15 were adopted, the first seven having been approved previously, when it was resolved that Duhamel be allowed the privilege of withdrawing section 17 with the right of bringing it in the following day in a separate bill. For this section, which referred to the colored militia, a substitute was prepared and passed which organized the militia into classes and provided for rotation of duty. (The prevention of possible further delay in the enactment of the militia bill appeared to have been the reason for changing section 17.) Sections 16, 18, 19, and 20 of the bill were then acted upon and finally, after some amendment, the measure passed on August 25 and was sent to the senate for concurrence.

On the twenty-fifth as agreed upon, Duhamel proceeded to the first reading of the bill authorizing the governor to enroll certain free people of color. On the following day the bill went through a second reading. At the third reading on Friday, the twenty-eighth, it was resolved on motion of Phillip Caldwell that the following be added:[69] ". . . provided, however, that the number shall not exceed four companies, and shall be persons possessing two years at least previous to their enrol (1)-ment a landed estate of the value of three hundred dollars or the sons of such persons." The bill was then voted upon and passed 12 to 2. It was entitled: "An Act to Authorize the Governor to Enroll Certain Free People of Color," and was sent to the senate the same day.

At the same time the senate was unable to agree on the regular militia bill. A joint conference committee was appointed which recommended certain changes. These were acceptable to both houses and the bill passed on September 4. It was then enrolled and forwarded to the Governor.

Meanwhile, on September 1 the senate returned the bill on the colored militia with an amended title which the house accepted two days later by a vote of 15 to 6. The house then enrolled the measure, notified the senate of its action, which acted likewise, and forwarded it to the Governor for approval.[70]

On September 5 the Governor returned the regular militia bill with a stinging veto. Claiborne stated that the bill as passed not only would throw the whole militia into a state of confusion, but contained some parts which were contradictory and others which could not be executed. Furthermore, the Governor said, in the present crisis it would prove hazardous to the public safety. His major objection was that the bill created officers upon whom large responsibilities rested, yet failed to provide for their nomination or appointment.[71] However, the day before, the Governor had observed that many sections of the measure were good and cautioned that leading principles of the militia system should be left untouched. There was certainly no need for radical changes, he felt, although some amendment was necessary to augment the authority of the officers.

The act concerning the colored militia had easier going: for one thing, it was less comprehensive than the other. The Governor approved it on Monday, September 7, 1812.[72] Entitled "An Act to Organize in a corps of Militia for the service of the State of Louisiana, as well as for its defense as for its police a certain portion of chosen men from among the free men of colour," it authorized the governor to form such a colored militia at his discretion. This corps was limited to four companies the strength of each to be sixty-four men including officers. Its personnel was restricted to free men of color "chosen from among the Creoles [sic]" who not only paid a state tax but who for two years previous had been the owners or sons of owners of landed property worth at least $300.00. The commander in chief was to provide for the choice of officers of the colored militia (with the requirement that their commanding officer be white) and be responsible for the manner of arming and disciplining the organization.

Governor Claiborne soon thereafter began the official reactivation of the colored militia which became known as the Battalion of Chosen Men of Color or more simply as the Battalion of Free Men of Color. Typical of the commissions which he issued was one for Isidore Honoré, a free man of color, whom he appointed second lieutenant in the battalion as of October 12, 1812.[73] It represents the first example of a state of the Union commissioning a colored officer.

Uniquely, this was the first time in the United States that a Negro volunteer militia with its own Negro line officers was authorized by state legislative enactment. But in one respect the state legislature simply had reactivated, with some modifications, an organization inherited from the Spanish regime in Louisiana. But under the American circumstances it was still unique; perhaps this could have happened only in New Orleans. It would be years before this happened elsewhere in America, and it would be generations before it happened again in the South. But whenever and wherever Negro military organizations would appear in the United States hereafter, until the mid-twentieth century, they would follow, especially in command, much of the same general pattern.

Meanwhile, the legislature resumed debate on the regular militia bill and was able to present one to the Governor which he found satisfactory and signed on February 12, 1812.[74] This militia act, composed of fifty-two articles, was a new one which repealed the territorial militia act of 1805 and the supplementary militia act of 1811. Section 1 restricted membership in the militia to white males, between the ages of sixteen and fifty. However, section 49 specified that the recent act organizing certain chosen free men of color into a militia was to be permitted. This was an omen for the future.

As far as overall regulations were concerned, the colored militia was governed by the regular militia act of the state, which in turn was guided and controlled by the national militia act of the federal government.[75] Regulations of the Louisiana act, which applied generally, concerned discipline, equipment, service, and pay. The colored militiamen as well as the other militia personnel were to be trained and exercised in a manner agreeable to the War Department and governed by its regulations. Failure to comply with the regulations in the strictest sense was punishable by fines and other means. Battalion reviews were to be held twice a year, once each in the months of April and September. Militia companies were to turn out on the last Saturday of each month, and at such times all militia personnel were to appear properly armed and accoutred. Militiamen were to serve within the limit of the state for a period not to exceed three months at a time. They were to receive while in such service pay and rations of militiamen in the service of the United States. The formal recognition of the volunteer militia of free men of color by the Louisiana state legislature was a definite but deserved victory for both the personnel of the organization and the Governor; it was also proof of the good judgment of the general assembly.

The state legislature, although open to criticism for passing a militia bill which in the eyes of the Governor was not entirely adequate, was not only following his advice but was at a great disadvantage in its first session, for it was involved in the innumerable details of organizing a state government. Committee appointments, contested elections, election of local officials as well as those for Congress, creation of the state court system, and other constitutional requirements had to be met, as well as the consideration for legislative enactment of matters duly brought before it. Paradoxically, at the very time that legislation for the organization of a colored militia was being discussed, favorable consideration was being given to masters seeking compensation for slaves who had met their death, or were imprisoned for life for participation in the recent slave insurrection.

On the other hand the attitude of those inhabitants of lower Louisiana who were opposed to the Negro militia is not difficult to see. The fear of slave insurrection was constant, and the possible accession of free people of color to the cauldron of insurrecting slaves was a calculated risk which many thought was not worth taking. Morever, the ever-increasing proportion of Negro to white made such ideas no less tenable. Louisiana business enterprise, in its development of an economy based on cotton, sugar, and steamboat traffic, depended increasingly upon slave labor thereby adding to the slave insurrection potential. Too, there was always the shadow of Haiti.

CHAPTER IV

ENROLLMENT INTO FEDERAL SERVICE

As INSPIRATIONAL as the establishing of the Battalion of Free Men of Color may have been to its personnel, to the free people of color of New Orleans and vicinity, and to the governor, it cannot be denied that events of the war influenced the favorable action of the legislature. War brought the battalion into the state militia and would next bring it into the United States Army.

Prior to 1814 the theater of operations of the War of 1812 was in the northern part of the United States. In that year, however, the British, repulsed in Baltimore after the burning of Washington and defeated in the overall action in the Lake War, were prevented from launching a general invasion from British North America. They then shifted their offensive to the south where an attack was undertaken against New Orleans. The overall objective of the project was to conquer and occupy New Orleans and the Gulf regions for the purpose of acquisition by the British, or at least to promote their independence from the United States. Failing this, possession was to be used as a factor in improving England's position at the peace talks which were already in progress in Ghent.[1]

That this was to be the final and decisive blow of the British against the Americans in the war was obvious from the heavy concentration of troops and equipment at the staging area, Negril Bay, Jamaica, British West Indies.[2] One British outfit after another was ordered there as they withdrew from Europe after defeating Napoleon in 1814 in the Peninsular War. In addition, troops already in America were transferred there or ordered to join the invasion forces enroute to New

56

Orleans. By November, 1814, the bay was literally covered with vessels, many of them ships of war, which carried collectively no less than a thousand guns. Apart from the large quantities of conventional material, there were Congreve recoilless rockets, seen by Americans for the first time at the Fort McHenry bombardment, and other supplies, testifying to the British attention to detail, such as printing presses and clothing for the anticipated allies. In addition, a number of nonmilitary personnel were aboard. Included were those who, hopefully, would become civilian officials of His Majesty's government after Louisiana was conquered.[3]

Of considerable interest is the fact that orders for the conquest of New Orleans and the Gulf regions were issued by the War Office after commissioners had assembled at Ghent to discuss peace. No wonder the British were not disposed to hurry discussion. In anticipation of the projected invasion, any delay would be to their advantage.

It was no idle rumor that Wellington, the Iron Duke himself, was offered the command of the expedition but declined. It was good that he did. Napoleon would return from Elba. But the offer no less was a tribute to the importance of the mission.[4]

Andrew Jackson in the same year was promoted to a brigadier of the line with a brevet of major general and assigned the command of the 7th Military District which included Louisiana, Mississippi, and what is presently the state of Alabama. He had received his promotion and assignment on May 22, 1814, but in less than a month, on June 20, was appointed major general to fill the vacancy occasioned by the resignation of Major General William Henry Harrison.[5]

A few months before, he had led his western volunteers against the Creek Indians who had perpetrated the Fort Mims Massacre in Alabama the previous year and defeated them disastrously at Horseshoe Bend in the same state. This success, coupled with his varied career on the local and national scene, made the popular Tennessee frontiersman a logical choice to command the American forces in the West against the British. In July, he was back in the Mississippi Territory completing the treaty with the defeated Creeks at Fort Jackson, after which he planned to go to New Orleans.

Jackson was not oblivious to the necessity of preparing the defenses of his district against the British. He comprehended the threat of the British to the area of his command in its entirety and felt that his defenses also included checkmating any potential British ally in his district. Indeed, Jackson needed no urging against the British. In the western part of Tennessee where he grew up, he came to believe, as others did, that Indian troubles and many kindred problems were due to machinations of the British. Nor did he eliminate from his mind the possibility of an Anglo-Spanish alliance in either the Southwest or the Southeast.

His suspicions of the Indians, Spanish, and British were not far from wrong. On July 21, while at Fort Jackson, he received a new British musket from a friendly Indian, who explained that he had been given the piece by Indians at Apalachicola Bay, Florida. This confirmed the rumor, Jackson thought, that the British planned to direct a blow at the lower country and were presently collecting arms and munitions and making allies preparatory for that.

On the same day he received the musket, he wrote Governor Claiborne that the capture of both Mobile and New Orleans and "exciting the black population to insurrection and massacre" would be possible objectives of the enemy. He informed the governor of his dependence upon Louisiana for aid which he trusted would be furnished promptly when required. In anticipation of this, he requested the Governor to hold in readiness fifteen companies of one hundred men each, officered and equipped in the best possible manner. These companies were to be organized from the militia of the state and were to be able to take the field at a moment's notice.[6]

By August 5, 1814, there was no longer any doubt in Jackson's mind as to the intentions of the British. They were not only increasing their supplies at Pensacola, but also were organizing and drilling fugitive Creek Indians, evidently with the consent and certainly with the knowledge of the Spanish governor. Jackson was now convinced that the British would use Pensacola as a base of operations against Mobile and New Orleans. He thereupon requested Governor Claiborne of Louisiana, Governor William Blount of Tennessee, and Governor David Holmes of the Mississippi Territory to prepare their militia for immediate active service according to the quota assigned on July 4, 1814, by the War Department.[7] According to this requisition, the quota for Louisiana was a thousand men.

Claiborne's reply to Jackson's first letter explained very frankly the unprepared state of defenses in Louisiana. He was most pessimistic and stated his honest opinion that if the state were then attacked, its security would have to depend upon the regular troops under Jackson's command and the western militia. Otherwise, Claiborne felt New Orleans would fall inasmuch as many of its points of defense were then unoccupied.[8] At the same time the Governor invited Jackson to visit New Orleans as he thought it would stimulate the inhabitants to defense measures. Meanwhile, realizing the effect of Jackson's name on the public morale, he took the liberty to publish part of Jackson's letter of the twenty-first.

Four days later, things appeared brighter in New Orleans. Claiborne was happy to inform Jackson by letter that in a recent interview with officers of the several militia corps he had been promised their co-operation in carrying out the general order concerning recruitment. The extent to which the public would support these officers, however, was a question. The Governor had great confidence in the Americans, the vast majority of the Creoles, and many Europeans of long residence in Louisiana and felt he could depend upon them. There were others, however, who were devoted to Spain and partial to England and upon whom he could not rely because they disliked the American government.

In the same letter, Claiborne went into considerable detail concerning the battalion of free men. After describing the militiamen and giving some statement of their virtues and difficulties, he told of interviewing their officers—Colonel Michel Fortier, the commander, a respectable and wealthy merchant of New Orleans; Major Pierre Lacoste, the second in command, a reputable and rich planter; and the officers attached to the companies, ". . . these last being men of color."[9]

During the interview Claiborne had "assured them that in the hour of peril, I should rely on their valour and fidelity to the United States."[10] In return they not only had expressed their devotion to their country and their readiness to defend it but also invited the Governor to organize and receive as part of the militia all the native free men of color of New Orleans and vicinity. They estimated their number to be near six hundred. It was felt that such action would give great satisfaction to these men and further secure their attachment to the American government. Governor Claiborne answered this request simply by ordering a census made of the free men and returned to him as soon as possible.

Claiborne cautioned Jackson that the manner of acting toward these men in the present emergency was a question of grave importance. If America did not use them, he believed the enemy would attempt to intrigue and attract them. Since they were accustomed to the climate, attached to arms, were of good character, and were property owners, the Governor felt that they would render significant service in that part of the country and in the event of invasion would be particularly useful. He believed a corps of three hundred or four hundred might easily be rasied which would willingly enter the service of the United States for six months, provided they could serve in Louisiana. Claiborne ended his communication by asking Jackson to what extent he felt authorized to receive such troops and his opinion as to the expediency of using them.[11]

General Jackson replied to Governor Claiborne on August 22, from four miles above Mobile where he had moved because of the increased danger from the British at Pensacola. Jackson's letter indicated that the pledge of support and patriotism displayed by the citizens, particularly by Colonel Fortier and the select corps under his command pleased him. On the basis of Claiborne's endorsement, the statements of the field officers, and the declarations of loyalty by the men themselves, he "would not hesitate in recommending that the corps be augmented" by an increase of the personnel of each company to one hundred rank and file.[12] These were to be held in readiness and counted as part of the militia quota required from Louisiana according to the recent order of the War Department. Jackson added, however, he could not promise to use the corps in the state alone. At the same time, he promised Claiborne a visit as soon as the safety of the area permitted.

Claiborne's strong recommendation of the Negro militiamen to Jackson was almost premature. The great majority were absent from parade on August 21, 1814, and the Governor was disturbed.[13] It was most unusual and not in keeping with their customary propriety. Those members, whose absence was neither authorized nor excused, had disobeyed the Militia General Order of August 18, 1814, which specifically ordered the muster of the Battalion of Free Men of Color twice every month.[14] Claiborne could not help wondering if some of the colored troops, like certain white militiamen, were becoming indifferent to the threatening crisis and Louisiana's militia quota.

Hearing that great discontent pervaded the organization, the governor called together the officers for an interview. They assured him that their trouble was local and rather of a personnel nature and was not directed against the government.[15] Although Claiborne was happy to hear this, he strongly suspected that Spanish or English agents had made overtures to some of the free men. He promised to investigate the entire affair and report to Jackson. Although no evidence supported any avowed disloyalty on the part of the men, the incident served to point up for Jackson what Claiborne already knew: the great difficulty of organizing the Louisiana militiamen to meet the quota. Too, it threw a bit of suspicion on the colored unit.

Meanwhile, Claiborne continued in his efforts to raise his quota but the results remained discouraging. While there were many faithful citizens in Louisiana, there were many who actually believed the state would pass to Spain. And some of this latter group doubtless felt that it should pass without a struggle in New Orleans just as in the old days when Louisiana was passed to one world power by another without the area experiencing the pain of the battlefield. Such a diversity of political sentiment existed among the Louisiana residents—Americans, French, Spanish, and English—that the Governor was persuaded that only a body of regular troops or of western militia would enable him to muster a corps of faithful Louisianians sufficient in number to satisfy his quota.[16]

Nevertheless, Claiborne persisted. Tightening his militia regulations as advised by Jackson, he was able to inform the latter, about the middle of September, that the only difficulty he had in the city of meeting the requisition came from some European Frenchmen. They had claimed exemption from the draft by pledging loyalty to Louis XVIII, King of France, through the French consul. Again he was quite pleased that the city militia had assumed the proper attitude toward the situation and was cheerfully performing patrol duty.

Although the urban population of New Orleans was responding to the requisition of the federal government, this was not true of the potential militiamen outside the city limits. A "Committee of Safety" wrote Jackson explaining that the excessive slave population, one white man to twenty-five slaves on plantations on both sides of the river from New Orleans to La Fourche, not only prevented the call of any white inhabitant to the frontier but required additional help.[17] The enemy had already attempted to incite their slaves and would, of course, repeat the attempt. Furthermore, following the same line of argument, the committee reasoned that the city militia could not be removed from the city limits. In conclusion, Jackson was informed that under these conditions his forces were depended upon entirely for Louisiana's external defense and to a great extent for domestic tranquility. A few days later, Claiborne confirmed the attempt of the British to arouse the slaves. He had taken the proper precautionary measures, however, and found the citizens very cooperative.[18]

Meanwhile, Jackson, having completed the treaty with the Creek Indians by the middle of August, gave fuller consideration to the defense of Mobile. Major William Lawrence, with a small garrison and twenty pieces of cannon, was ordered to occupy the hitherto neglected Fort Boyer which commanded the entrance to Mobile Bay, some thirty miles below Mobile.[19] Jackson scarcely anticipated the British. Four days later they landed 600 Indians and Spaniards in addition to 120 marines preparatory to attack. On September 12, the British fired on the fort to no avail. The British reinforced two days later by three ships, fought a marine and land battle with the small American force which lasted some hours. Despite heavy odds, Lawrence was able to repulse the enemy with slight losses: four men killed, five wounded, and two cannons lost. The enemy loss was estimated at not less than eighty-five killed and wounded aboard the British ship *Carron* alone.[20]

Jackson next planned to attack the British at Pensacola, where the British had not only sent reinforcements but had hoisted their flag along with that of the Spanish over the forts there and had invited all Spanish citizens and Indians to join them. He immediately sent for the Tennessee militia troops which had been so closely identified with him in his war against the Creeks to assist him.[21]

About this same time, September 21, he rushed to Claiborne a number of dispatches designed to unite the Louisianians in face of the common danger and complete the organization of the militia. Claiborne was to publish certain of these dispatches and vividly emphasize the significance of the British attack on Mobile. Written for wide appeal and to obtain large numbers of volunteers, the covering letter began epigrammatically with "Our Country has been invaded and threatened with destruction. She wants soldiers to fight her battles."[22]

This communication particularly referred to the colored militiamen. Agreeing with the Governor that their background and experience would make them "excellent soldiers" and that they would not be idle spectators in the present crisis, Jackson went on to say that confidence should be placed in them. By so doing "you engage them by every dear and honorable tie to the interest of the country who extends them equal rights and privileges with the white man."[23]

Jackson enclosed an address (to be published) to the free people of color, which he hoped would stimulate enlistment among them. Jackson conceived of the approach as an experimental one. If Claiborne succeeded in raising a regiment, battalion, or even a company, he was directed to inform the general immediately in order that he could send one of his aides to organize them and pay them their bounty.[24] This would immediately place them on the same footing as soldiers procured by enlistment.

Jackson also enclosed an address of similar purpose to all the citizens of Louisiana. Copies of the address and several British proclamations, signed by Colonel Edward Nichols and naval Captain W. H. Percy, which invited the Louisianians, Kentuckians, and Baratarian privateers to join the British ranks, were published also. These enemy proclamations, it was hoped, would show the British in their true light. Jackson also informed Claiborne that he had begun recruitment of the Choctaw Indians and soon hoped that he would have a sufficient force to take the offensive and humble the "overgrown pride of the British." [25] Claiborne received the correspondence and enclosures from Jackson on October 17, 1814, and promptly published all except the one to the free men of color which he did not release until later in the month.[26] This delay was occasioned by the alleged distrust of the white citizens of the unit and a misunderstanding between officers of the battalion. So great was the whites' suspicion (which the Governor thought was totally unwarranted) that it was doubtful the ensuing legislature would renew the battalion already organized.

Arguments concerning it had been most extreme. Some opposed it outright and wished for its climination; others believed the only way to prevent the armed Negro men from becoming allies of the enemy was to place them on equal footing in every respect with white citizens; this was, of course, prohibited by the state constitution. However, by the twenty-eighth the differences between the officers and men had been settled, the loyalty of the free men of color seemed assured, and a spirit of moderation had been restored. It was not until this time that Claiborne felt justified in publishing Jackson's appeal to the free men of color.[27]

This address "To the Free Coloured Inhabitants of Louisiana" was directed to the patriotism of that group and encouraged them to enroll in the service of the United States. It carried high motivational appeal. Referring to the colored inhabitants as "brave fellow Citizens . . . sons of freedom" and as "Americans," the general invited them "to defend our most inestimable blessing . . . to rally around the standard of the Eagle, to defend all which is dear in existence." [28] Jackson desired to impress on the free men that their service was not only wanted but needed; he left no doubt of this for he noted that he addressed them "in the sincerity of a Soldier and in the Language of truth." Moreover, he denounced as a mistake the policy which heretofore had deprived them of participation in the "Glorious struggle for National rights." [29]

The speech had its practical side also, for Jackson spelled out the manner in which he planned to use the Negro militia. Although it would operate as a separate unit under white officers, the noncommissioned officers would be drawn from its own ranks. Jackson used this arrangement to enable the colored corps to pursue "the path of glory" as "a distinct, independent Battalion or Regiment" which would deter criticism and unjust comparison with the white troops rather than set up, unwittingly or not, military segregation, as some have suggested.[30] At the same time, General Jackson promised the members of the Negro militia the same treatment and the same rewards which would be accorded white soldiers. This included not only pay, rations, clothes, and bounty money but also 160 acres of land.[31]

In his planned organization and utilization of these colored troops, however, Jackson had left nothing to chance. Instead, he displayed caution not devoid of some uncertainty. After all, he had neither seen nor fought with these troops and had only Claiborne's partisan word to go upon. Informing Claiborne that the jealousy of the citizens toward the free people of color was an activating motive in his address to them, he quickly added that only their pride and merit entitled them to confidence should they be used against the enemy. On the other hand, if there were any doubt as to their loyalty they were to be removed to a position where they could neither injure the American side nor aid the enemy.[32] Whether the colored militiamen were aware of Jackson's precaution is unknown. Even if they were, it made little difference, for Jackson's speech was both an invitation and a challenge.

Jackson's address was quite effective. Claiborne reported that A. M. Bourgeois, a Frenchman who claimed residence in the United States, said he could raise a company of a hundred Negroes provided he would be commissioned their captain.[33] Two other gentlemen also desired to raise companies among the free people of color. Moreover, the response of these people was enthusiastic. Equally favorable was the reply of the white citizens to their special address.

On November 5, 1814, the governor assured Jackson the state's requisition of a thousand infantrymen would be completed soon. When the cavalry and riflemen were added, Louisiana would have an auxiliary force of twelve hundred men. Although the enthusiasm and response did not yet compare with that of western states like Tennessee and Kentucky, Claiborne sensed the growth of a strong hatred toward the enemy and a great determination to unite in the defense of the country. These results he attributed largely to Jackson's addresses and the anti-American proclamations of the enemy.

While the organization of the militia was going on in New Orleans, Jackson assembled his forces and moved against Pensacola. After the Spanish governor was unable to guarantee the neutrality of Pensacola, Jackson virtually took the city by storm. Shortly thereafter, after completing the security of the Mobile–Pensacola area, the General left for New Orleans, on November 22, 1814.

As a result of his observations, he had become convinced that if an enemy attempted to invade New Orleans, it would have to be by Lake Pontchartrain.[34] Concerning the latter point, future events would prove whether he underestimated the British. Before leaving for New Orleans, Jackson had ordered General John Coffee with two thousand of his militia brigade from Tennessee to march to New Orleans and cover it until the militia from West Tennessee and Kentucky, which had also been sent for, could reach that city.[35]

The effect of Jackson's arrival in New Orleans on December 2 was electric; the people of Louisiana were inspired anew. Jackson spent the first day in the city attending to social amenities, reviewing the volunteer companies, and collecting information concerning the protection of the city. On the following day, he set up headquarters in the city and announced that he would necessarily be absent for a few days.

As a result of his personal inspection, he ordered Fort St. Philip (San Felipe under the Spanish) strengthened by two additional batteries so placed as to effect a deadly cross fire to an enemy approaching New Orleans by the Mississippi from the Gulf. In addition, he promised guns for an installation in process of construction at English Turn, eighteen miles below New Orleans on a prominent bend in the river. Finally, he directed the installation of a battery at Chef Menteur, the waterway which leads from Lake Pontchartrain to Lake Borgne, about eighteen miles northeast of the city.[36]

General Jackson was not a bit too soon in hastening to New Orleans and attending to his defenses. The enemy task force, some thirteen thousand strong in some fifty ships, had left Negril Bay for New Orleans about the same time Jackson left Mobile for the city. General John Keane was commander-in-chief of the British expedition and Vice-Admiral Alexander Cochrane was in charge of naval operations.

By the tenth the British had anchored in the deep water between Cat and Ship islands in the northern waters of the Gulf of Mexico at the head of Lake Borgne and had begun to transfer troops to smaller vessels to navigate the lake. On the fourteenth the British defeated the small flotilla of American gunboats on Lake Borgne. They then began the serious debarkation of their troops at Pea Island at the mouth of the Pearl River.[37]

Jackson learned of the capture of the gunboats as he returned to the city on the fifteenth. He immediately ordered every assailable approach to the city fortified or obstructed. Major Lacoste with his militia battalion of free men and the men of the Dragoons of Feliciana were immediately assigned the security of Chef Menteur Road which crossed the plain of Gentilly leading from the city to the strait connecting Lake Borgne and Pontchartrain.[38]

Captain Vincent (Vass) Populus, the ranking Negro officer of Lacoste's battalion, upon receiving from Major Lacoste the disposition of the colored troops, took immediate action to bring them together. By December 16, 1814, Captain Populus had notified all members to assemble early on the day following, ready to march to Chef Menteur. His own company was told to report at 4 A.M., December 17. Populus' order disrupted somewhat the work program of certain officers of the United States army such as Captain C. L. Humphrey of ordnance, who employed two blacksmiths belonging to Populus' outfit and needed their services at the time they received orders.[39]

Whether Humphrey's request to detain the men was approved is not known. Orders were orders. The Battalion of Free Men of Color consisting of four companies, marched to Chef Menteur under the immediate command of Major Lacoste on December 17. Maximillian Brulé, the proud *porte drapeau,* carried the American flag and the battalion ensign high that day. He was leading the outfit to active duty not for France or Spain, as he had before, but for the United States of America.[40]

The group took position at the confluence of Bayou Sauvage and the Chef Menteur River. Major Lacoste was specifically ordered to erect a redoubt at this terminal point and oppose the enemy who, Jackson felt, would attempt an approach from that direction.[41] The Major was furnished with two brass field pieces which were to be used until twelve-pounders should be sent. The assignment was one of vital importance for it not only controlled the Gentilly approach to the city, but also the lower approach to Lake Pontchartrain which gave access to the city. It was a responsibility of honor and trust and reflected the confidence General Jackson had in the colored battalion.[42]

Meanwhile, Jackson took other measures. Special messages were expedited to General John Coffee, General William Carroll, and General Philemon Thomas notifying them of the loss of the gunboats and ordering them to hasten to New Orleans with their commands. General James Winchester at Mobile was alerted, and Washington was notified to send arms. The services of Baratarian privateers were offered and accepted. Authorization was given to levy and organize into companies all the friendly Choctaw Indians. New Orleans was declared under martial law and a levy *en masse* was proclaimed.[43] Those troops still in the city were to pass in grand review on the *Place d'Armes* (Jackson Square) in front of St. Louis Cathedral on Sunday, December 18.

The levy *en masse* proclaimed by General Jackson brought about the official enrollment of the Battalion of Free Men of Color, as well as certain other militia organizations, in the service of the United States. Technically speaking, some of the units were already performing services for the United States under the orders of Jackson. Major Lacoste's battalion had already been ordered to Chef Menteur. Captain Ferdinand Lioteau and his company of Negro militiamen, who were drafted for six months and had been sent on December 8 with Major Walter H. Overton to Fort St. Philip, were officially enrolled into the service of the country as of December 12, 1814.[44] But the original Battalion of Free Men of Color (four companies and two companies added subsequently) were now officially mustered into the service of the United States and became part of the United States army on December 16, 1814, with the exception of Lioteau's company, referred to.[45]

At that time, the first Battalion of Free Men of Color had an aggregate strength of 353, including an eleven-piece band and staff officers.[46] Vincent Populus was the ranking Negro officer with a grade of second major or aide major. This was the first recognition by the United States Army of a colored officer of or near field grade, indeed, of one with superior rank. On many occasions Populus was in charge of the organization, although Major Lacoste was the commanding officer.

The companies which composed the battalion with their aggregate strength were those of Captain Louis Simon with seventy-one, presently commanded by Lieutenant Maurice Populus; Captain Charles Porée's with sixty-three; Captain Antoine Diesses' with fifty-four; Captain Basile

Demazelliere's with fifty-one; Captain Jean Ternoir's with forty-eight; and Captain Ferdinand Lioteau's with forty-five.

Of these companies none was more proud or hidebound in tradition than the one later identified with Captain Louis (Jack) Simon. This was the first company of the first Battalion of Free Men of Color. It was one of those authorized by legislative enactment of September 16, 1812. At that time it had volunteered its service to the state and was accepted for the duration of the war.[47] Vincent Populus was captain then, and it was a grenadier company which had had its origin during the Spanish period.

On December 1, 1814, Populus was elected second major and became teaching instructor when the battalion was expanded prior to entry into the service of the American government. Maurice Populus, its first lieutenant, then became acting commander of the company which position he held until Simon was named captain. The company seemed like a Populus organization, for the roster listed eight individuals with that surname, some of whom probably were related. Of these, two were commissioned officers, two, noncommissioned officers, and four, privates. Maurice Populus, it will be recalled, was among those who signed the petition to Claiborne in 1804. Barthelemy Populus became the second Negro militiaman of rank in the organization; on December 15, 1814, he was appointed adjutant in the battalion, with the rank of first lieutenant.[48]

François Chartry, the former white adjutant of the battalion, became adjutant, with the grade of captain, of Colonel Fortier's entire regiment which was now in process of formation. Other men whose names appeared on the rosters of the several companies of the battalion had signed the petition to Governor Claiborne and had seen service under the Spanish flag also. Among these were: Charles Porée and Jean Ternoir, captains; Baltazare Demozeillier, first lieutenant, and Jean Dolliole, Voltaire Auguste, Louis Daunoy, and Pierre Bailly (father and son), all of whom were privates.

Sometimes the military tradition of a family extended to the reception of a commission by the son of a former distinguished officer. Such was the case of Noel Carrière, first lieutenant in Captain Demazelliere's company. His father was Noel Carrière, former sublieutenant under Gálvez (by whom he was decorated for service against the British in 1779), who later became captain and commander of the colored militia near the end of the Spanish control of Louisiana.

Some names were reminiscent of even earlier military experiences of the Negro in Louisiana. For example, names like Simon hark back to Bienville's war with the Chickasaws, while Bailly (father and son) is the same name as that of the director of affairs for the Company of the West at Natchez who together with his son were fatalities in the 1729 massacre. Finally, Lachaise is the elided surname of councillor De la Chaise who originally recommended the organization in New Orleans of the company of free Negroes for military use at the time of the Natchez troubles.

Such was the personnel of Major Lacoste's Battalion of Free Men of Color of Colonel Fortier's regiment. Its history ran deep into the past and it was rich in both tradition and experience. No wonder it was called the battalion of "the chosen men of color." These soldiers had accepted their assignment with anticipation of doing their part and of receiving military benefits and fuller rights as citizens and they expected action. This was the surest way to justify their traditions and realize their aspirations.

Besides this regular battalion of free men there was another group who answered the call to service on the sixteenth. These were men of color of the city and vicinity, forty-five and older, who were not liable for active duty but responded for service with other older men in the home guard, whose duty was more of a police nature. Seventy-nine of these free men of color were formed into a company under the command of Gabriel Gerome, a venerable colored man of the community. Few were armed, only twenty-seven pieces being distributed among the entire number.[49] Some of these men were assigned to Major Daniel Hughes at Fort St. John, at the mouth of Bayou St. John and Lake Pontchartrain. Among them was a detachment of eleven free men under Corporal John Pierre Labau, who was referred to as Captain Labau or Labaud. Surnames like Dorville, Rochon, and Esclavon, reminiscent of Spanish days, also appeared here.

General Jackson was so impressed by the original Battalion of Free Men of Color that, soon after seeing it, he expressed the desirability of raising another comparable organization. This turn of events was most welcome to Claiborne, who had originally suggested and had continuously advocated the idea to Jackson. Colonel Fortier, who would be their superior officer, also received the idea with great enthusiasm. The actual recruitment of personnel for this second organization was carried out by Joseph Savary, a free man of color from Santo Domingo, who had earned a distinguished reputation as an officer in the French Army during the war there.[50]

He volunteered his services and virtually singlehanded raised a
second battalion from among the free Negro émigrés from Santo Domingo, most of whom had fought as loyalists under the French flag in
their native land. It was a herculean task, but Savary procured sufficient personnel and Claiborne and Fortier cooperated—the latter
summoned Savary and the outfit to his house for enlistment—in such
a manner as to have the organization or a large part of it ready for
the review.

On the eighteenth, as scheduled, General Jackson reviewed those
troops remaining in New Orleans. Included were the city militia, the
uniformed battalion of Major Jean Baptiste Plauché, and part of the
regiment of men of color. Inspiring speeches were delivered to each of
these as they were drawn up on parade. To the units of free men of
color still in the city, Edward Livingston, now aide to the General, read
Jackson's address.[51] In the main it was a laudatory speech. Reminding
the Negro militia members that he had called them "to arms" from
Mobile "to share in the perils of war and to divide the glory" with their
white countrymen, the General said he had expected much from them
as he was aware of those qualities which made them "formidable to an
invading foe," but they had surprised him and surpassed his hopes. He
found in them those qualities united with the kind of "noble enthusiasm which impels great deeds." Expressing pride in them and praising
them for their ardor, he informed the groups that he would apprise
the President of their conduct on this occasion so that he, too, as the
voice of the American nation, could applaud their valor. Jackson concluded by calling attention to the immediacy of the situation and the
task at hand, "the enemy is near; his 'sails cover the lakes'; but the brave
are united; and if he finds us contending among ourselves, it will be for
the prize of valour and the rewards of fame." [52]

The second Battalion of Free Men was mustered into the service
of the United States on December 19, 1814, the day following the review. When enrolled, the organization had an aggregate strength of
256, including staff officers.[53]

Joseph Savary, who had recruited the volunteers, was the ranking
Negro staff officer, with the rank of second major. Savary's grade
and function compared to that of Major Populus, as a white officer
was attached soon after its organization. But there was a difference—
Savary had the unique distinction of being the first Negro man appointed to the rank of second major in the United States army. Jackson had recognized the appointment of Populus but he, himself, had

appointed Savary to that grade. This is revealed in the change which the General authorized on the muster roll of this organization. On the muster roll of the staff officers of this battalion opposite the name of Savary in the rank column appears the word "Major" written heavily over another word, apparently "captain," which was partially removed. The word "Major" is preceded in a different handwriting by a lightly written "2nd." In the remarks column written heavily like the word "Major" is the statement "By order of G. Jackson." [54] The date of Savary's appointment is December 19, 1814. Jackson was indeed impressed by the manner in which Savary raised his troops.

The second battalion was composed of four companies, each of which had white officers commissioned as commanders. This, of course, was different from the practice in the first battalion and reflected the organizational scheme concerning white commissioned officers and Negro troops that Jackson mentioned in his first speech to the free men of color. This arrangement helped to establish procedures for organizing Negro troops as separate units that remained in practice in the United States until mid-twentieth century. The aggregate strength of each company and the names of their officers commanding were: Captain Charles St. Martin with sixty-seven, Captain T. C. Lefevre with sixty-four, Captain Berlin Rouzier with sixty-two, and Captain Marcellin Gilot with fifty-three.[55]

The rank and file personnel of this outfit had been most responsive to the call for men to fight the British. In the case of the Bonseigneur family, which had come to New Orleans from Haiti, no less than four brothers—Paul, Caesar, Detterville, and Jean—answered the call to colors. Later, Jean was found to be too young to serve as medical aide and became messenger and orderly to Captain Lefevre.[56]

Even though this organization or some part of it appeared in the parade of the eighteenth, it was neither completely organized nor equipped at this time. But within forty-eight hours after muster it was ready for action. By the twentieth, its personnel had been armed with "good muskets" from the state's store, stood inspection, and expressed an anxiety for duty.[57] On the following day orders directed the issue of their other equipment.[58] Major Louis D'Aquin, an officer of the 7th Regiment and an émigré from Santo Domingo (who had been an officer under the French Republic), was attached to the battalion as its commander.[59] His surname was soon popularized into Daquin.

The new outfit, 253 men including officers of the Negro corps, was to be sent to Chef Menteur, but Claiborne reminded Jackson on the twenty-first that its members were ill prepared for a winter campaign as they were thinly clad and had no blankets.[60] Claiborne felt because of this they would not move out as expeditiously as he wished; he also informed Jackson that he had no more funds for such purchases. He was willing, however, to make such purchases on joint credit with Jackson deductible from the pay of the battalion. On the next day, however, blankets were provided for the men through the generosity of Colonel Fortier. Claiborne then pointed out the need of shoes. The colonel again came to the rescue and furnished four hundred pairs of shoes at personal expense that same evening.[61] Meanwhile, events were so shaping as to demand the service of the outfit elsewhere.

Jackson, optimistic and encouraged by the overall response to his efforts, continued performing the innumerable details connected with preparedness. Colonel George T. Ross was directed to apply at the Magazine Barracks for arms which had been recently brought down-river by Colonel William Carroll. General John Coffee and his troops had arrived, as had Major Thomas Hind's and were both encamped within a short distance of New Orleans. The Choctaw chiefs and warriors were enrolled. Captain Peter Ogden with a detachment of soldiers was ordered up the coast for the purpose of apprehending subversives. He was to inquire specifically after the conduct of slaves and search all places where it was thought they might have collected arms for insurrections.[62] The two twelve-pounders with the necessary ammunition were ordered sent to Major Lacoste's colored battalion at Chef Menteur.[63]

CHAPTER V

IN THE BATTLE OF NEW ORLEANS

GENERAL JACKSON'S PREPARATIONS were interrupted about noon on December 23 by the news that the British had landed not at Chef Menteur where Lacoste and his colored troops awaited them but on the Villeré plantation about nine miles below the city. There, General John Keane, with the assistance of Admiral Cochrane, landed an advance section of about two thousand men.[1]

With the landing of the British officially confirmed, Jackson announced to his headquarters the decision to fight the British that night. Within an hour the troops in and around New Orleans within a five-mile radius were all in motion under special orders. General William Carroll's detachment of Tennessee militia and the city militia commanded by Governor Claiborne, with the exception of Plauché's and Daquin's outfits, were stationed four miles above the city to meet a second attack from Chef Menteur where firing had begun earlier.[2]

The remainder of the forces—Major Daquin's Battalion of Free Men of Color, 210; Major Plauché's battalion of uniformed companies of militia, 287; Major Hind's dragoons of Mississippi riflemen, 107; General Coffee's brigade of Tennessee volunteer mounted rifles, 563; parts of the 7th and 44th regulars with 465 and 331 men, respectively; and Colonel McRae's artillery detachment numbering 22 and 18 Choctaw Indians were ordered to Rodriguez Canal, six miles below the city, preparatory to meeting the enemy.[3]

This grass-grown canal, twenty feet wide and four feet deep, was an abandoned millrace on the old Macarty plantation. It was now a dry ditch which ran perpendicular to the levee and the woods. It was to be-

73

come Jackson's base of operations and behind it he later would erect a breastworks. It would place him two miles from the enemy position, which extended about a half mile on the river and in the rear nearly to the woods.

Actually, there was no single continuous line of march of Jackson's troops from the city as some outfits were more distant from New Orleans than others. But by 2:30 that afternoon some units had already formed below the city ready to proceed to Rodriguez plantation. At 5:00 Jackson, after attending to last minute details, followed General Coffee who had been ordered to take position to the left of the De la Ronde house if he did not meet the enemy. Jackson led a detail with two six-pounders and the 7th Infantry Regiment.[4]

Of those going to meet the British that evening none was more thrilled than the fully uniformed drummer of the 7th Regiment of regulars who, though only a "teenager," rolled his seemingly oversized drum like a veteran.[5] He was Jordan B. Noble, a free Negro boy from Georgia, who came to New Orleans early in the war and joined the 7th Regiment as drummer boy in 1813 at the age of thirteen. Noble had been extremely busy since Jackson had issued marching orders on the twenty-third, for in those days the drummer executed many of the beats, signals, and calls now associated with the bugle and whistle. Presently, after conducting a detachment of the 7th from Fort St. Charles to the old barracks on Levee Street, where another part of the regiment joined them, this drummer boy was leading them to meet the enemy.

On his way to De la Ronde's in support of Coffee, Jackson was met by his intelligence officer who informed him of the details and the disposition of the enemy. Upon arriving at Rodriguez, the General became aware that the British, who were still landing troops, planned to encamp. Moreover, he found that instead of preparing for battle, other than posting pickets, the enemy set about improving their camp and indulged themselves in a holiday mood. In their relaxed mood, the British even permitted the armed American vessel *Carolina* to move downstream opposite their camp.[6]

On the American side, Jackson gave his full attention to immediate preparation for battle. He personally supervised the planting and protection on the levee road of the battery brought with the troops he personally led. After forming the 7th Regiment on its left, he charged the adjutant general with the formation of the other troops upon their arrival in the following order: Plauché's battalion to the left of the

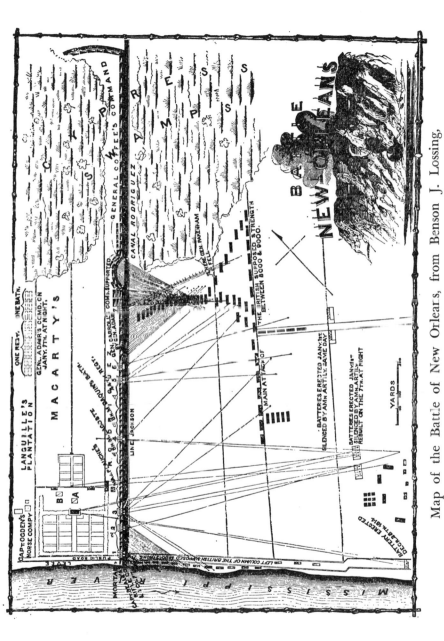

Map of the Battle of New Orleans, from Benson J. Lossing,
The Pictorial Field-Book of the War of 1812 (New York, 1869).

7th, Daquin's Negro battalion on the left of it, and the 44th on the left of the line.[7] Jackson's strategy was intended to be one of deception. This formation was intended to deceive the enemy whom, Jackson hoped, would suppose that "our best troops in the center would attack the flanks." [8]

Jackson then left to examine Coffee's position, after which the two officers checked the enemy position for the best possible plan of attack. The plan agreed upon was a simple one. Jackson would attack the enemy front, Coffee, their rear, while Patterson rained broadsides from the *Carolina* in the river. To this end, General Coffee with the left wing, 732 strong, was sent to attack and turn the enemy right by an encirclement movement. Jackson at the same time leading the right wing, nearly fourteen hundred strong, was to attack the enemy's strongest position, the left nearest the river.[9] The overall operation as first planned called for deployment and uniting both wings before the enemy. Firing from the *Carolina* would begin the action.

The vessel drew nearer to the bank and swung broadside. Commodore Patterson passed the firing order. Seven guns responded, spreading death, destruction, and pandemonium throughout the British camp. Jackson, having waited the half hour for the full effect of the broadsides, ordered the advance.[10] As his troops moved forward, however, a shift in position began to occur which ultimately placed the 44th in the center and Daquin's colored battalion on the flank, left of the line with Plauché's troops between.[11] The order regarding deployment and uniting had been ruled out in the final plan. But most of the organizations of the right wing received the change too late, if at all.

With the exception of the 7th Regiment, Jackson's troops formed from their first position and marched in extended line instead of columns. As they moved forward, the area in which they maneuvered became diminished because of the curve in the river on one side and the De la Ronde house, on whose right they were to operate, on the other. The 44th and 7th advancing in the dark, yet with the briskness of regulars, unavoidably squeezed Plauché's and Daquin's battalions out of line and to the rear while they themselves joined together.

By this time a company of the 7th had advanced as far as the boundary of Lacoste's plantation when an outpost of the British opened fire.[12] The Americans returned fire and spirited fighting followed with each side giving and regaining ground. Other troops of each side took position and soon a battle line began to emerge, the advantage with the British because of their constant reinforcements. Engagement became general. The British line soon outflanked the American left, which it manuevered to turn.[13]

Turning the American line seemed imminent. Already the 44th had been compelled to oblique on the left to prevent this. The British, sensing this weakness, were sending more soldiers to execute the flank movement. It was at this critical juncture that Plauche's battalion, Daquin's colored battalion (now led by Joseph Savary), and a small band of Choctaws joined the line.[14]

Momentarily Plauché's troops crowded the regulars of the 44th and fired on them; but they were quickly posted properly and directed their fire on the enemy. The colored troops made contact with the British when "the enemy column advancing in the dark fell suddenly almost within pistol shot of the extremity of Daquin's battalion and commenced a brisk firing." [15] Militia and regulars, now joined, restored the American line, and forced the enemy to give ground.

General Coffee with his left wing had accomplished his mission.[16] Not only did he repulse the enemy, but he also forced them to retreat to the river side of the levee. At this point, Jackson's order to cease fire ended the night battle.

The fighting of December 23 came to an end. Both commanding officers soon turned to their casualty reports. British General Keane reported 46 killed, 167 wounded, and 64 missing, a total of 277.[17] General Jackson reported 24 killed, 115 wounded, and 74 missing, a total of 213. In Daquin's battalion, one captain and six men were wounded.[18]

General Jackson was jubilant and believed that his inferior forces could have destroyed the enemy if it had not been for the fog. However, the fog may have saved him from disaster. He reported that the whole corps under his command deserved the greatest credit and praised each outfit individually. Of the Negro battalion he said; "Savary's volunteers led by him under the command of Major Daquin, showed great bravery." [19]

Although the British did not consider the engagement of the twenty-third a real defeat, there is no doubt as to its importance to America. Actually, it saved New Orleans. Jackson pointed out, and not without logic, that if the British had not been attacked with such impetuousity when they landed, they would have successfully marched against the city.[20] This would have been disastrous, as the city was neither fortified strongly nor adequately defended. Moreover, the action not only gave Jackson's troops self-confidence, but also forged white, black, and red men, many of whom were raw militiamen with different cultures and languages, into an effective military weapon.

As time went on, armchair strategists presented many arguments as to why the British were prevented from taking the city on the night of the twenty-third. One which gained great popularity was the failure of the enemy to turn Jackson's line because of the performance of the Louisiana militia troops. The Louisiana *Courier*, referring to the battle three years later when a greater calmness for discussion existed, stated: "The arrival of the battalions of Major Plauché and Daquin on the field was, perhaps, what saved the country for they met the enemy when he was about to turn the 7th and 44th Regiments of the line in which he must have inevitably succeeded notwithstanding the bravery of the two corps had it not been for those battalions of from 600 to 700 men." [21] Legendary as this became for home consumption, there is no doubt that all of Jackson's troops were responsible for the repulse of the British that night.

Sometime during the day of battle, Jackson took time to express himself as to the treatment of his soldiers. Although specifically directed to apply to the Choctaw recruits, there is no doubt that what he said was to be interpreted comprehensively and concerned with policy in case the question might arise again or if there were further doubts. It was occasioned by the assistant district paymaster's (at Mobile) questioning Jackson's policy of paying the Choctaw Indians. Jackson replied in a pointed order that left no doubt of its meaning. "It is enough," he pointed out, "for you to receive my order for the payment of troops with the necessary muster rolls without inquiring whether the troops are white, black or tea." [22] In spirit and idea it ranks with other comparable statements by American officials in their attempts to extend the fundamental meaning of democracy to all.

More pertinently for the free men of color it was a harbinger of the future. The assistant paymaster was advised to keep to himself thereafter his opinions upon the policy of making payments to certain troops. The paymaster was not to know whether Jackson had received authority from the War Department to employ any particular description of men and, upon receipt of this communication, was immediately to make payment to the Choctaws upon the muster rolls of Major Uriah Blue deducting only the amount noted for clothing. The general reminded the officer that he had already stated the necessity of making prompt payment to the Choctaws and concluded, "Let it not, therefore, again be necessary to reiterate this order." [23]

On the twenty-third another organization of free men of color officially appeared on the scene. This was the company of a Negro officer, Captain Charles Forneret, which was recruited that day at Fort St. Leon on the west bank of the river where it was stationed as garrison troops.[24] It was a small company mustering about thirty-one the day it took post. Later others would join, swelling the number to forty-one. Many of the men were from outside the city limits and had answered the call for troops issued by Jackson on the twenty-second which called residents of outlying areas to service. The organization was part of the Louisiana militia under the command of General David Morgan. Fort St. Leon, whose defenses they were to help prepare, was in a most neglected state of repair at the time.

The next action with the enemy did not occur until December 28. Between the twenty-third and that day both sides strengthened their positions. Leaving the 7th Infantry and a company of dragoons at De la Ronde's as an outpost, Jackson withdrew his main forces to Rodriguez Canal where the men proceeded to throw up entrenchments thirty yards in the rear. Tools were requisitioned from the city, and all available men were set to work widening the canal and throwing dirt on the bank nearest the city. By the end of the twenty-fourth Jackson's entire line was protected by a mound three or more feet high. On the extreme right, the two six-pounders which had been used the day before were placed in battery to control the road.

On the very same day, December 24, 1814, the treaty of peace between Great Britain and the United States was completed and signed at Ghent by commissioners of the two nations. However, during the discussion and negotiations of the treaty, which had been going on since August, the British had outfitted and dispatched the expedition against the United States under temporary command of General Keane, as has been seen.

But on Christmas Day, Lieutenant General Sir Edward M. Pakenham, colonel of the 7th Foot Regiment, Royal Fusiliers, arrived in the British camp to take command of the troops as previously planned.[25] Pakenham, brother-in-law of the Duke of Wellington of Peninsular War fame and later the hero of Waterloo, was himself an officer of renown. He carried the battle scars of a number of campaigns; for his bravery in the Peninsular War, he was called the "Hero of Salamanca." Now in his late thirties, he commanded a British army most of whose regiments had fought triumphantly under Wellington. Many, like the 85th, 44th, and 21st regiments and the 14th Dragoons, had established laudable reputations. They were to be joined by the 40th, 43rd, and Pakenham's own 7th, all of whom were expected hourly.

The War Office had earlier explained to Pakenham that he was to cooperate with His Majesty's fleet and was to "preserve the best understanding between the military and naval forces" employed in the operation against New Orleans.[26] He was not told that he was to wage offensive warfare on a low, open plain against troops fighting defensively from behind strong breastworks whose flanks were protected by the river on one side and the swamp on the other. Major General Samuel Gibbs, colonel of the 59th Foot Regiment, also an experienced and distinguished officer, came with Pakenham as second in command.

On the same day, amidst his preparations at Rodriguez, Jackson received a verbal report that the enemy had landed at Chef Menteur, and that Major Lacoste, who commanded the post at the confluence of Bayou Sauvage and Chef Menteur River, had abandoned his position and removed his Negro battalion and camp three miles back on the Lafon plantation.[27] This report and Lacoste's movement alarmed all the forces on Gentilly road, as an attack appeared imminent. General Jackson immediately ordered Major Latour to hasten with a detachment from General Coffee's brigade under the command of Colonel Nick to the abandoned post.[28] The colonel was to take command of the post of Chef Menteur, reoccupy the position, and complete the closed battery of Major Lacoste. Besides, he was to post a detachment in the nearby plantation to cover the retreat if such were necessary and to maintain communications with the city. The matter of executing these orders was left to the Colonel, and Lacoste and Latour who were to cooperate. Latour was also to investigate and report Lacoste's action to the general.

At the same time Jackson sent a stinging communication to Lacoste. He pointed out that he had been informed that Lacoste had retired his command at Chef Menteur at the approach of the English and thereby abandoned ground that easily could have been defended. He continued, "You must take a stand, Sir. The Battery you have under your command must be defended to the last extremity." In addition, he pointed out that he had placed great confidence in the Major, and "the valour of the troops under your command, let me not be deceived." Furthermore, he informed Lacoste that the British had attacked there on the twenty-third but had not been able to advance "one step" and that the troops had covered themselves with glory. This was a noble example to follow—"no more retreating." Adding that he had sent reinforcements which would give Lacoste every advantage of position, he concluded with a final admonishment, "Let it not be said that the English had on their side the courage." [29]

Meanwhile, Lacoste had written to Jackson explaining his action. Their communications probably crossed. The major explained that the movement of the enemy necessitated his change of position. British soldiers had been seen in the area. Some had set fire to the dry grass which gave the impression that a landing would be attempted in that vicinity. In order to prevent being intercepted in the rear, he had changed to a new location. [30] Lacoste had left a picket at the former station who was to inform him of the enemy movements at Chef Menteur.

Lacoste was deeply injured by Jackson's reprimand. Not only was it a reflection upon him but upon his outfit also. For the first time in its long history, the word "retreat" was associated with the Battalion of Chosen Men of Color. It could not afford such a blot upon its escutcheon, nor did it think it deserved such. The reputation of the outfit had to be cleared. With this in mind, Major Lacoste returned to headquarters with Major Latour to discuss the matter with Jackson.

Jackson apparently accepted Latour's report, substantiated by Lacoste's explanation, for he granted permission to the latter to form his battalion on the line at Camp Jackson. [31] There was no doubt that the men wanted action. It was reported they exercised extensively at Chef Menteur. From nine to eleven A.M. on December 22, Claiborne said he not only heard continuous firing on Gentilly road but counted seven heavy guns. [32] Upon inquiry, he learned it was the Lacoste outfit probably simulating an attack. Was it really mock warfare? Was Vass Populus deliberately trying to attract or scare the enemy? Whatever the reason, the original Battalion of Free Men of Color was on its way to Jackson's front line (they called it "ligne Jackson"), where the battle was actually fought. It was where their sister battalion which had already seen action and had earned Jackson's commendation for bravery was stationed. The original battalion wanted such an opportunity also.

Meanwhile, Jackson strengthened his line with the addition of five cannons. These he placed in four batteries. Battery No. 1, two six-pounders, mounted the levee. No. 2, a six-pound howitzer, covered the river road, and Batteries Number 3 and 4, two twenty-four pounders, were about fifty yards from the road.[33] The last two cannons were furnished by the privateer, Laffite, and his Baratarians. In addition, the American vessel *Louisiana* which was pulled to safety when the *Carolina* was blown up by the British on the twenty-seventh was now anchored so that she could sweep everything in front of Jackson's line.

Such was Jackson's line against which Pakenham led his troops on the morning of December 28, only to be repulsed by the "deadly fire" of the guns of the Louisiana and Jackson's line. Pakenham had intended the operation to be a reconnaissance in force that would awe and probe the enemy line. But Jackson's artillery and the guns of the *Louisiana* were so effective that not only were the British stopped in their tracks, but also three of their field pieces were dismounted and several artillerists were killed. But the reconnaissance was not without its lesson to Pakenham. He learned the effectiveness of Jackson's guns, the futility of hoping to frighten Jackson's line into flight, and the need of a new plan to defeat the Americans.

The result was a plan to breach Jackson's defenses by heavy artillery from the Navy and then carry the American line by assault with Pakenham's infantry. To this end, Admiral Cochrane ordered the transfer of almost a score of the Navy's large guns to the field of battle. By New Year's Day, after arduous operations, the British mounted no less than twenty-four guns for siege tactics.[34] The British army had taken the field on the night of December 31, preparatory to carrying the assault as soon as the breach was made.

Meanwhile, Jackson, anticipating the enemy, continued to strengthen his line. By December 30 his line mounted a total of fifteen guns, including three across the river.[35] Not the least of the American emplacements was the thirty-two pounder mounted in the center of the line that became Battery No. 4.

New Year's Day on Jackson's line was greeted with a parade which got under way after inspection as soon as a thick fog began to thin. There were the American regulars, of both Army and Navy, American sailors, Louisiana Creoles, Louisiana Americans, free people of color, American frontiersmen, Baratarians, Acadians, citizens of France, and Choctaw Indians in almost as many different uniforms, many of which were nondescript. It is not improbable that the band from Lacoste's Battalion of Free Men of Color helped furnish the music as did Jordan and his drum, as bands were reported to have played, both "Yankee Doodle" and the

"Marseillaise" on that occasion. Maximillian Brulé was all the more proud. He was a color bearer on Jackson's front line.[36]

Before the parade ended and just as the fog lifted, the British artillerists commenced firing. For fifteen minutes they fired with "unexampled celerity," striking the Macarthy House for ten minutes with approximately a hundred balls and shells and Jackson's center of the line with an even heavier bombardment.[37]

More startled than confused, Jackson's line soon regained composure. When the smoke cleared away, the defending artillerists, taking careful aim, returned the enemy fire with target accuracy. The carefully aimed balls of Jackson's artillery repeatedly scored hits. Moreover, they easily penetrated the light fortifications of the enemy including the hogshead of sugar used in building the installation. Especially effective against the British were the Baratarians' twenty-four pounders and Crawley's thirty-two-pounder, Batteries Numbers 3 and 4. The former, according to British Captain Hill, "did us by far the most damage," but the latter, including the "giant redshirted mulatto who sponged out the gun after each shot" impressed British Quartermaster Surtee as he watched through his glass.[38] Its fire power was directed against the British main battery. Shortly after three P.M., the battle was over with every British battery silenced. The British troops waiting for the assault signal once more were ordered to retire.

The British reported seventy-eight casualties—thirty-two killed, forty-four wounded, and two missing. This report covered the period from the first to the fifth of January, but mainly reflected the battle of the first.[39] The American casualties were thirty-four, of which eleven, mainly from the artillery, were fatalities.[40] Of the total, one lieutenant, one sergeant, and one private of Daquin's battalion were casualties.[41] In his terse report to Secretary of War Monroe, the jubilant Jackson praised all his troops collectively. The "tremendous cannonade" of the enemy "was sustained by every corps under my command with a firmness which would have done honor to veterans." [42]

But Pakenham and Cochrane faced the challenge with firmness: the American line would be assaulted by storm. There would be some change in tactics. A strong detachment would be sent to the west bank in an effort both to capture the American big guns and then use them to sweep the American line before the main assault began.

While preparations were being made to implement these plans, Major General John Lambert arrived with reinforcements. The British forces now numbered near ten thousand, a force formidable enough to awe any body of troops at the time. They were divided into three brigades under Gibbs, Keane and Lambert.[43]

Meanwhile, Jackson continued to improve his work behind Rodriguez Canal. By the seventh, the rampart built on the town side of the former canal measured about a mile and a half in length from near the river to the impassable part of the swamp, five feet in height, and twenty feet thick in some places, while in others it would hardly stop a cannon ball.[44] Everyone had taken part in building it. Isidor Sandos, private, Captain Demazelliere's company, of the first Battalion of Free Men of Color, found the work so novel and arduous that he insisted on digging in gloves.[45] This earned for him the nickname "Gant" by which he became so popular that it followed him the rest of his life. Jackson assigned the responsibility of the defense of the west bank to General David Morgan and his militia troops, while he concentrated in the east bank where he believed the main attack would be made.

As finally arranged, his line in general followed that of the twenty-ninth and first except it was stronger. It was composed of eight batteries of fourteen guns strategically placed. These batteries in turn were covered by the infantry which they were to support. The Negro troops defended the fourth battle station on Jackson's line on the east bank the morning of the eighth. Major Lacoste's battalion of free Negroes, 280 strong, joined Plauché's militia troops to its right. Major Daquin's battalion, numbering 150, followed Lacoste's group and joined the 44th regulars to its left.[46]

Battery No. 4, the thirty-two pounder, twenty yards from No. 3 and one hundred and ninety yards from No. 5 was commanded by Lieutenant Crawley of the United States Navy. It occupied the interval between the two colored battalions whose fire it was to support. This, the largest gun on the line, had been very effective in the artillery battle of January 1. Its protection was the responsibility of Major Daquin's troops shared by those of Lacoste. Troops and battery together made this one of the strong points on Jackson's line. Daquin's troops defended, besides the battery, the line half the distance to Battery No. 5, where it was joined by the 44th regulars.

Altogether the troops and artillery mentioned made up Jackson's right on the east bank. It was commanded by Colonel Ross and numbered about 1,400, nearly equally divided between regular and militia troops. Of these militia troops, all from Louisiana, four hundred, (over half), were local Negro militiamen. Jackson's center on the east bank was composed of Tennesseans and Kentuckians and the fifth through the seventh batteries, under the command of General Carroll; while his left, extending from the center to the impassable part of the swamp, was commanded by General Coffee and composed of Tennesseans. All in all, Jackson's troops totalled slightly more than 5,000, of which slightly more than 4,000 were on the east bank of the Mississippi.[47] Of the latter, about 3,200, including the colored troops, were on the firing line, while about 800 were posted strategically behind it.

Such was Jackson's main line of defense and the position of his main forces on the eventful morning of January 8, 1815. Negro drummer boy Jordan B. Noble had beat an early reveille that morning and the long roll had every man at his post.[48]

As ordered, the British troops had taken their position preparatory to assault before dawn. The chief attack was to be made against Jackson's left near the edge of the woods by the second brigade led by General Gibbs, while General Keane would demonstrate against the other part of Jackson's line.[49] General Lambert with the third brigade was in reserve. The noise of the attack on the west bank, to which a column commanded by Lieutenant Colonel William Thornton had been sent, was to be the signal for the attack. But it never came. The current of the Mississippi had upset the column's timetable. The troops landed late and at a point not intended.

Pakenham, impatient with delay and disappointed at losing the advantage of surprise, decided to attack. Even though he was informed by General Gibbs that the 44th had forgotten the fascines and ladders necessary to fill the ditch and mount the ramparts and that three hundred men had been sent for them, the General gambled.

Assuming that the detachment and equipment would be in place in time, he signalled the attack.[50]

A thick fog, in addition to the smoke from the bombs and rockets covering the advance, permitted the British to advance within seven hundred yards of Jackson's entrenchments before discovery. Upon discovery, Gibbs's advance was met by a most galling fire from the batteries. Numbers 7 and 8 were ordered to cease firing so that the troops of Carroll, Coffee, and Adair could pick their targets, but the batteries in the center continued their destruction.[51] When they were within three hundred yards of Jackson's line, the western militiamen fired with deadly accuracy. The British column was broken and torn. Still it tried to advance, stumbling over casualties and firing without order and aim. Disorder soon gave way to confusion which Pakenham, who rushed to the front, was unsuccessful in disspelling. General Keane, realizing the plight of the main column, ordered his column to its aid. Blasts of grape furrowed the ranks as it obliqued across the field. The thirty-two pounder was most devastating. Then once more blazed the fire of the Tennessee and Kentucky rifleman.

The main assault of the British had been completely repulsed. It was a disastrous defeat. Within an hour the attacking British had lost their commander and two brigade generals who had been mortally wounded and about two thousand troops who were casualties.[52] It was no wonder that General Lambert, seeing the carnage as he moved his troops up, asked for a truce and later a cessation of hostilities, despite the eventual success of the British on the right bank.

Jackson's losses from his line at this time were only six killed and seven wounded.[53] Losses from a skirmish in the field which followed would increase this total. All thirteen casualties on the line were from the 7th Regiment and the Tennessee and Kentucky militiamen. Jackson's success was all the more notable because it involved no more than one half of his infantry line on the east bank. The battalions of Plauché, Lacoste, and Daquin and the entire 44th Regiment on the right and one half of Coffee's Tennesseans on the far left were not under direct enemy fire inasmuch as the assault was not general.[54] Besides, the American small arms were ineffective beyond four hundred yards.

Joyous as Jackson was over the immediate victory, he was disappointed at the conduct of his troops on the west bank. The battle across the river had gone against the Americans. The British had finally landed and surprised Morgan and his men into a hasty retreat which extended about a mile and a half before the line could be reformed.

The retreat did not include Forneret's company of Negro troops, however.[55] For this unit remained stationed as garrison troops at Fort St. Leon from December 23, 1814, to February 14, 1815. The location of this fort removed it from threats of the British forces inasmuch as a large swamp intervened between it and the attacking enemy. By the time Morgan had reformed his troops, Lambert had recalled Thornton because of heavy adversities on the east bank. The whole affair became anticlimactic.

While the action on the west bank was in progress, events on the east bank took a turn which led to a skirmish on the field as had been indicated. The repulse of the British had lasted less than an hour. Jackson's infantry troops had ceased firing by 8:30 A.M., although his artillery continued intermittently to answer the British large guns until 2 P.M. Over a thousand British troops had been left wounded on the field. Moreover, many able-bodied troops had fled to the ditch and swamps in order to escape injury.

Now, at the end of firing, many of the Americans left the ramparts without orders to go upon the field to help the wounded and take prisoners. Many British soldiers were captured and taken to the American line. Those who were wounded were given prompt medical aid by the American medical staff. In some instances, the Americans carried the severely wounded to their line on their backs. To those too injured to be moved they gave water and tried to ease their suffering. This humane treatment of the enemy wounded was especially touching and was watched with feeling by troops remaining on the ramparts.

While engaged in such activities, a group of the free men of color was fired upon by a party of British soldiers in the ditch. One Negro was killed and three severely wounded.[56] This action was considered an outrage by the Americans and caused considerable excitement in their line, for the colored soldiers were not only engaged in an act of mercy but were said to be unarmed.

Later the British soldiers would attempt to explain their conduct as an error of judgment. They claimed they could not understand the language of the Negroes who had come to their assistance, and thinking they came to murder and steal, fired upon them.[57] It has been charged that they were fired upon by order of some of the lesser British officers out of the mortification of their defeat. There was no doubt that the British resisted capture. Their defeat had been most humiliating, expecially to their officers.

The operations of the Americans became increasingly more difficult, for the British not only began to recover their own wounded but sought to prevent the Americans from taking prisoners of war. A detail of British sharpshooters came to life on the field and began picking off Americans with great success.[58] Indeed, the Americans suffered more casualties after the main action than during it.[59] They were definitely at a disadvantage. Only after the removal of the sharpshooters could they venture upon the field and continue to take prisoners.

Captain Joseph Savary, who was among the most fearless of the courageous officers and men defending the American line, immediately sensed the stalemate and offered a solution. He was granted permission to lead a company of free men of color, which he was commanding in Daquin's battalion, upon the field for the purpose of dislodging these soldiers. A small skirmish followed on the field, but Savary accomplished his mission and the snipers were eliminated.[60] In so doing, however, his company suffered ten casualties. Savary's brother, an ensign, besides three sergeants, one corporal, and five privates were wounded.[61] It was a daring and brave act, entirely beyond the call of duty, and added further laurels to Daquin's battalion.

The Baltimore *Niles' Weekly Register* was particularly impressed by this mopping-up action of the Negro troops. In its account of the battle of January 8, it reported that "the killed and wounded on our part were chiefly of the New Orleans colored regiment who were so anxious for glory that they could not be prevented from advancing our breastworks and exposing themselves. They fought like desperadoes and deserved distinguished praise." [62]

Savary's operation was the last significant action between the troops on Jackson's line although the Americans resumed firing at four that afternoon, when a two-hour truce ended. Not until the following morning did Jackson, upon receiving a second note from Lambert, issue a cease-fire order. The first had been returned for proper signature indicating authorization and status. But for all practical purposes, taps, beaten by Jordan B. Noble at the end of the battle day, closed this phase of the attack on New Orleans.

The American casualties for the eighth were seventy-one, of which thirteen were fatalities, thirty-nine, wounded, and nineteen, missing.[63] Of this total, fourteen were from the Negro organizations. One private was killed and three were wounded in Lacoste's battalion. One commissioned officer, four noncommissioned officers, and five privates were wounded in Daquin's battalion.[64] The enemy reported 2,037 casualties. Of these 291 were killed, 1,262 wounded, and 484 missing, many doubtless taken as prisoners.[65]

Meanwhile the British had opened another attack, not at Chef Menteur, however, but at Fort St. Philip. On January 9 an enemy squadron of five ships had reached the fort but found its defenses too powerful to pass. Anchoring out of range, it began a bombardment.[66] The attack on Fort St. Philip alarmed the command at Fort St. Leon into frantic preparation. If the British got by Fort St. Philip and its supporting works, Fort St. Leon would be next and then New Orleans itself.

What made the work of preparing the defenses of Fort St. Leon frustrating, if not outright demoralizing, to Forneret and his men stationed there, was the fact that up until December 26 they had been feverishly preparing the fort for action and then on that day they were ordered to stop and prepare it for abandonment. General Morgan, as has been seen, had been ordered to fortify and defend a line on the west bank opposite Jackson. The order for abandonment called for leaving a small force at Fort St. Leon and removing all large armament. Those pieces which could not be transferred were ordered to be sunk in the river, to be retrieved when necessary.[67] Now, Forneret's outfit and the others were to restore the defenses of the fort with great urgency.

Captain James H. Gordon, with rank of brigade major, was assigned command of the fort January 4, 1815, and ordered to complete its defenses.[68] By the eleventh he had mounted two cannons on the left near the levee and had erected a hot shot furnace; at the same time he asked Jackson for artillery pieces and experienced artillerists.[69] With the help of his hard-working garrison, including Forneret's Negro troops, Fort St. Leon at last began to assume defense status. By the eighteenth, with additional supplies and a total of 235 men, the fort was defensible.[70]

But Fort St. Philip withstood the bombardment, and although damaged, was not captured. Finally on the eighteenth the British, convinced of its impregnability, withdrew. The Americans suffered casualties of two killed and seven wounded. This was from a garrison of 366 under the command of Major Overton. Among other units included in the garrison was one of thirty free men of color under Ferdinand Lioteau, who had been helping prepare the defenses there since early in December.[71]

The participation of the Negro troops in the defense of New Orleans was a significant moment in the history of the Negro race in the United States. One battalion with Jackson met the British when they first landed, participated in the attack, and was subsequently assigned a position on the front line of defense which it held throughout the entire campaign. The other battalion at first performed reconnaissance duty in a key sector and then was given a front line position which it defended throughout the remainder of the campaign.

Interesting is the fact that, during part of the time at the front, Savary commanded Daquin's Battalion of Free Men of Color and that Lacoste's outfit had colored line officers. For leading a detachment to clear the field of enemy snipers after the main action, Joseph Savary is also worthy of citation for performance beyond the call of duty. His band of soldiers also deserve meritorious recognition. All in all, the performance and attention to duty of the personnel of both organizations were creditable. Each suffered casualties including fatalities; Ensign Savary died January 10, 1815.[72] And along with other troops on the line, both groups were commended by Jackson.

Officially there were no desertions from troops on the line, although there were three absences.[73] These were one absence with permission, one absence without leave, and one unexplained absence. The first two were from Captain Demazelliere's company but in the final recapitulation only one is recorded and that as missing. The other absence was from Captain St. Martin's company. Two desertions occurred in Lioteau's company and five are accredited to Forneret's outfit. In the case of the former they are recorded as of December 13, 1814, one day after the unit had entered the service of the United States and ten days before the first engagement of Jackson with the enemy at Chalmette. In Forneret's organization only three are actually listed as deserting, although five appear in the summary on the back of the roll. It is quite possible that the other two are included among the ten who were sick, all of whom were absent. Even so, these three desertions are dated after the enemy action against Fort St. Philip.

Certain northern states were watching the experiment with the colored soldiers in Louisiana, and some, like New York and Pennsylvania, decided to create such organizations. But they were never comparable to those of Louisiana. None had colored line officers, let alone field officers. New York, however, did include some arrangement wherein slaves could move toward freedom through enlistment. But Louisiana, in comparison with the rest of the country, was unique. The Louisiana Negro militiamen emerged from the war as America's pre-eminent colored soldiers and first such elite corps. Moreover, they afforded a significant precedent for the organization and utilization of the American Negro as military personnel. But even more important, they illustrated to the United States and to the world that colored men, when given the opportunity, made combat soldiers second to none.

CHAPTER VI

AFTERMATH OF VICTORY

THE BATTLE OF NEW ORLEANS was over; the enemy had been repulsed and the city saved. Participation in the battle had been the most significant military experience of the colored corps in its long history. Soon after the departure of the British, Jackson decided to break camp and return to the city. He had already requested Abbé Louis Guillaume Dubourg to arrange for a public thanksgiving service at St. Louis Cathedral in honor of the event.[1]

Before leaving for the city on January 21, 1815, the General publicly complimented and thanked the corps which had served under him in the defense of the city. He told the two Negro volunteer corps that they had "not disappointed the hopes that were formed of their courage and perseverance in the performance of their duty," that Major Lacoste and Major Daquin, their commanding officers, "deserved well of their country and that Captain Savary continued to merit the highest praise." [2]

The troops eagerly anticipated a quick demobilization and return to civilian life. But Jackson was not willing to endanger his victory by a premature dismissal of his men. He had received no official information from Washington that the war was over, and he was well aware that the enemy might attempt another attack from some other point. Therefore he informed his troops to remain alert and ready to return to active duty at a moment's notice. The special orders for the companies of Major Plauché's militiamen and for the colored battalions of Lacoste and Daquin returning them to the city, specifically provided that each outfit was subject to drill once each day by its commander and was to hold itself in readiness to march at any time.[3]

After assigning units to guard certain vulnerable points as a precautionary measure, Jackson returned to the city with the main body of his troops for the first time since the beginning of the campaign. The reception by the populace was overwhelming. After the impressive thanksgiving service, the remainder of the day and night was given over to festivity. But on the following morning practically everyone was surprised that martial law was again in effect and that troops were being assigned duty as if the war were still on and New Orleans were in a state of siege. This was precisely what Jackson intended. Demobilization and the restoration of civil law were far from his mind, for the enemy was yet entirely too close. Furthermore, the General was responsible for the security of the 7th Military District of which New Orleans and Louisiana were only a part.

Nor was he wrong. The enemy, on its outward voyage, had laid seige to Fort Boyer where Major William Lawrence was still in command, and after two days of fighting, the fort surrendered on February 9, 1815. Moreover, Admiral Cochrane had received a communication from the British War Office which he interpreted as requiring him, along with Major General Lambert, to continue hostilities against the United States until he was notified that the treaty had been officially ratified by America.[4]

However, many Louisianians were unable to appreciate Jackson's point of view. Numbers of militiamen refused recall to duty and whole outfits deserted their posts. Reasons for this action were not difficult to find—New Orleans had been saved and the enemy had fled. They felt, therefore, that their mission was accomplished. Moreover, their families and occupational pursuits required them. Too, since the battle of the eighth, camp life had become very unhealthy because of inclement weather; some soldiers had died from pleurisy, and the sick list continued daily to mount at an alarming rate.[5]

Furthermore, the soldiers and civilians were unable to obtain from Jackson any commitment concerning a date of dismissal from service. His reply to Claiborne, who had written regarding this on January 31, ignored that subject for the present and instead complained about the dereliction of duty of several Louisiana militia corps at Camp Villeré which had been recently vacated by the enemy. Incidentally, on this occasion, Claiborne offered his services, in his civilian capacity, to treat with the British relative to the slaves who had been carried off.[6]

This only annoyed Jackson, and he quickly informed Claiborne that it was his responsibility to deal with the British concerning the slave question. Certainly, from this time on, if not before, the militia problem became involved in the conflict between martial and civil law.

Meanwhile, the general assembly by joint resolution of February 1, 1815, took full notice of the manner in which the citizens of Louisiana and the troops conducted themselves during the invasion and thanked them for their patriotism and bravery. Colonel Fortier, Major Lacoste and Major Daquin, and Captain Savary, along with the battalions of free men of color and the free colored women in the city who served as nurses, received special praise.[7]

It appeared that many of the troops took this as a benediction for desertions, and absenteeism increased. Soldiers of French nationality who had just recently served under Jackson used a different method to avoid further duty. They applied to Chevalier de Toussard, the French consul at New Orleans, for certificates of French citizenship which automatically exempted them from further service. This official was as cooperative in granting these as he had been enthusiastic in encouraging the Creoles and Frenchmen to enter the war under Jackson.

At first Jackson was not too disturbed at this procedure and even countersigned the certificates thereby approving their exemption. But as the number increased, he soon discovered that it was a means to evade further military duty and realized that if this procedure were allowed to continue, it would demoralize his troops and reduce their numerical strength.

There was no doubt that the example of Frenchmen shedding the army so easily influenced other militiamen to quit the ranks. Nor was it improbable that some of these ex-soldiers encouraged their former comrades in arms to return home. It is unjust, however, to charge them with the entire breakdown of military discipline because this had earlier set in. But it was a contributing factor. As the rate of defection increased, it became apparent that all groups were affected. There was no appreciable difference in the percentage of deserters from the ranks of the white troops than from those of the colored.

This action was not true of all these troops, just as it was untrue of all French soldiers. Major Lacoste's outfit had responded to Jackson's latest call for further duty. And General Jean Humbert's *Legion des France* (organized about February 9, 1815) had thirty-one colored men along with forty-six white men, presumably French and Creole, and fifty-five Spanish, under Captain Bourgeau at Camp Villeré on the twenty-third.[8] Some of the Negro men were from Daquin's organization.

But part of this battalion was guilty of insubordination. On February 15, 1815, General Robert McCausland, then in charge of part of the militia, ordered Major Daquin to proceed with a detachment of his troops to Chef Menteur where they were to improve the fortifications.[9] This was purely fatigue work, however, and the detachment refused to go. When Daquin inquired why, the men not only reaffirmed their decision not to perform this type of duty but requested him to inform the General that "they would always be willing to sacrifice their lives in combat in defense of their country as had been demonstrated but preferred death to the performance of work of laborers." [10] Some of Daquin's men eventually reported to Chef Menteur where part of Lacoste's battalion was already stationed. But Captain Savary, who wrote the letter, remained steadfast and refused to march his men from the city.[11]

Savary's strong statement and his steadfastness, along with that of his detachment, helped further to establish the image of Negro soldiers in Louisiana as combat troops. Savary and his detachment had created the image on the battlefield. Now they had risked military censure and punishment to preserve it, and they got away with it. But Savary had taken a great risk. He was too able an officer not to have realized that his action was indefensible as far as military discipline was concerned. Only his record and Jackson's indulgence saved him.

However, the effectiveness of the men from both battalions at the post was seriously impaired by wholesale absence without leave, or actual desertion. Major Daquin reported that 144 men were absent from the two organizations on February 20.[12] Four days later, he informed General McCausland that something had to be done or else there would be no privates left.[13] In addition to the several reasons mentioned, perhaps these men, especially in Daquin's battalion, knew that Jackson was trying through Claiborne to raise a quota of slaves from nearby planters to work at Chef Menteur. Claiborne did not have much success in this at first, and the soldiers interpreted their being ordered there as an insult.

Meanwhile, Claiborne wrote Jackson again on February 24 urging the dismissal of the militia.[14] Jackson answered that he was mindful of the unrest of the soldiers and would return them to their homes as soon as possible without endangering the safety of the country.[15] He was doing all in his power to accomplish this and had already contacted Admiral Cochrane regarding the cessation of hostilities as based on the treaty of peace, of which the British officer had been informed but of which Jackson had not. Jackson reminded Claiborne that the Tennesseeans were steadfast in duty and suggested that they be used as an example for the Louisiana militia.

The day before, however, Claiborne had recalled Stephen Murureau, attorney general of the state, to his official duties, regardless of Jackson's martial law. The Governor instructed Murureau to be prepared to aid civil magistrates in the defense of the rights of private citizens not actually in military service.[16] Claiborne was rather exasperated with matters as they stood and pointed out that he no longer could be an idle spectator of the prostration of the laws of the state. The actual invasion had ended; yet martial law was continued, he lamented, to the great injury of the rights of the citizens.

Military breakdown continued. Mutiny was rumored from Fort St. Philip. Jackson now decided to get to the bottom of the entire situation. On the twenty-eighth, he issued an order requiring the removal to Baton Rouge of all former soldiers who had acquired French citizenship through certificates which he had signed.[17] This was a security measure and despite much protest the order went into effect. The 3rd United States Infantry, Major Plauché's battalion, the two battalions of free men of color, and Captain Beale's rifle company, all under the command of Lieutenant Colonel Arbuckle were assigned the duty of enforcing the order on March 5, 1815, the final deadline, against all those who had not complied with its requirement.[18]

Jackson had really opened a hornet's nest. Louisiana, especially New Orleans, was still predominantly French, and whether Creole or continental, this element of the population had played a conspicuous part in the defense of the city. The General soon felt the reactions to his decree. An article appeared in the *Courier* of March 3, attacking him for the retention of martial law and the treatment of French citizens.[19] The article bore no signature, but Louis Louaillier, a distinguished and popular member of the legislature who was a naturalized citizen from France, quickly acknowledged its authorship.

On the fifth of March, Jackson ordered his arrest and trial by court-martial.[20] When United States District Judge Dominic Hall issued a writ of habeas corpus for the legislator, the judge was arrested and later removed beyond the confines of the city at Jackson's orders.[21] And when the United States district attorney presented a writ for the judge, he also was arrested.[22] On March 6, Toussard, the French consul, despite his claim of diplomatic immunity, was removed from the city for opposing Jackson's measures.[23]

On the same day a special courier from Washington bearing news concerning the ratification of the treaty arrived in New Orleans. By some mistake, however, he had left Washington with the wrong dispatches. Nevertheless, on the following day Jackson softened. Taking a different approach to the situation, he ordered the dismissal of troops.[24] He explained that he had only been waiting for a plausible reason for such action and felt that, although he had not received official confirmation of peace, the strength of persistent rumors justified his action.

Too, he did not want to tax the patriotism of the inhabitants, yet he warned them to be prepared for recall to duty if the need occurred. He further advised them to beware of the intrigues of those who were envious and disappointed and sought to undermine the military. Actually, Jackson dismissed only some of the troops at this time. Among the troops he retained in service were the battalion of Major Plauché, the Negro battalions of Daquin and Lacoste, and the rifle company of Captain Beale.[25]

On March 8 Jackson suspended also the order which had removed the French subjects. This was done at the several requests which he received from the officers serving under Plauché, Lacoste, and Daquin. They had personally guaranteed the proper conduct of the persons involved. The suspension, however, excepted Toussard, who was required to obtain a special permit to return to the city.[26]

Finally, on March 13 official news arrived from Washington that the Treaty of Ghent had been accepted and peace was restored between the United States and Great Britain. Jackson now ordered the dismissal of troops, the revocation of martial law, and the general pardon of military offenders. In his farewell address to the soldiers, Jackson praised them highly, but did not fail to take a parting shot at his civilian critics. He emphasized that while real danger was before them he had not found it necessary to be severe with any of his men, but that after the enemy had retired, improper actions of certain individuals compelled him to resort to strong measures. In so doing, however, he reminded his fellow soldiers that he had been careful to punish the guilty and not the innocent, "the seducer rather than the seduced." [27] From now on, the Louisiana troops were dismissed from the service of the federal government and returned to the command of Governor

Claiborne. Not until March 30 were all the militia finally under state control.

Major Daquin's and Major Lacoste's battalions were mustered out of the service of the United States government and returned to the jurisdiction of the state of Louisiana on March 19 and 25, 1815, respectively.[28] Organizational payroll records of the War Department show that the several captains received pay at the prevailing monthly rate for their company personnel.[29] Commissioned officers were also paid at the prevailing scale for that class including a monthly allowance for a servant. In addition, Vincent Populus and Joseph Savary, each of whom received the pay of major, got allowances for one private and three horses for each officer.[30]

Jackson's lesson to the paymaster before the battle had been well learned. There was, as the General promised in his first address to the colored soldiers, no discrimination in pay based on race. The federal government treated all of its soldiers alike.[31]

The period of time for which the personnel of the first battalion was credited was three months and nine days, while that for the second battalion was three months and one day. Lioteau's outfit, as indicated, was given credit for a longer period as it had entered service a few days earlier. The only unit of free men of color which served less than three months was Forneret's. It was discharged March 11, 1815, after two months and nineteen days of service.

Certificates for faithfulness to duty, which amounted to honorable discharges, were issued by Major Daquin to the soldiers of his battalion. These were signed by the Major and also by Andrew Jackson.[32]

It is likely that Lacoste followed the same procedure but not to the extent that Daquin did. For one thing, his men were the last to be dismissed and were anxious to get out of service. Officers were also issued honorable discharge certificates. That of Barthelemy Populus stated that "he had behaved with courage and fidelity in the defense of New Orleans." [33]

Soon after the return of the colored militia to the state, its members began to display an increasing indifference to the organization, which led to its decline and contributed to its passing. This occurred in spite of varied attempts to revive enthusiasm and arrest its decline. At first nothing seemed amiss. Certain changes had taken place in the top echelon of officers but they did not appear too disturbing. Colonel Fortier, who had done so much in organizing and equipping the battalions, resigned his command and was succeeded by Major Lacoste, who

HEAD-QUARTERS,

7TH MILITARY DISTRICT OF THE U. STATES,

New-Orleans, March 20, 1815.

By Major-gen. ANDREW JACKSON,

commanding the said district.

BE IT KNOWN that *Barthelemy Populus* has served as a lieutenant in the company of coloured volunteers, commanded by ~~████████~~, in the campaign of 1814-15—That he has behaved with courage and fidelity in the defence of New-Orleans against the invasion of the British army, and has received an honourable discharge.

In witness whereof, I have hereunto set my hand and seal, the day and year before mentioned.

ATTEST,

Honorable discharge certificate for Barthelemy Populus, signed by Andrew Jackson.

was promoted to that position with the rank of lieutenant colonel on October 4, 1815.[34] Major Plauché took the position formerly held by Lacoste.[35]

Fortier, who had been the senior officer of the original battalion since territorial days, was now advanced in years. A review, perhaps the last of the colored corps under his orders, was scheduled for July 30, but was postponed until November 12, 1815.[36] At this time it was held under its new commander, Lacoste, who like Fortier, had been connected with the outfit since its earliest days.

Under this officer the battalion made plans to participate in the commemoration of the Battle of New Orleans, which had been celebrated before, but in which the free men of color had not always been invited to take part. On January 8, 1816, the first occasion, they were requested by their commanding officer to meet on the public square at twelve o'clock to commemorate the event. They were to be in full uniform and were to be provided with twenty rounds of blank cartridges.[37]

But in the period which followed, the decline became quite obvious. On September 16, 1816, a week after Claiborne had noted the general disorganized state of the militia corps and ordered their improvement, he specifically directed the Negro battalion not only to muster twice a month but to complete their organization without delay through volunteer enlistments. The Governor at the same time notified the officers that they were expected to place the battalion in the best possible condition. In concluding his directive, he informed the colored militiamen that the Governor "persuades himself that the corps of whose conduct in peace and war, he has had such satisfactory evidence will continue to deserve the highest confidence." [38] This was, perhaps, Claiborne's last official compliment, though a backhand one, to the corps, as he died the following year. His death marked the loss of the last of the three strongest and most influential friends of the colored militia. Jackson had gone elsewhere, and Fortier had resigned. Too, many of the able colored leaders were aging.

In compliance with the Governor's demand, the battalion on September 25, 1816, was ordered to muster twice a month and to complete the strength of its various companies by recruitment.[39] The same order was issued again on November 16, 1816.[40] Enthusiasm continued to lag, however, and the outfit failed to muster full strength.

Jean François Chatry, former adjutant major of the colored militia, was promoted to major and given command of the organization on March 28, 1818.[41] As late as 1825, however, he had not been able to bring the organization to permanent full strength. He issued a special order on March 14, 1825, authorizing the captains or officers of the four companies to complete the strength of their units.[42] Little came from this, however.

When the free men of color presented themselves to Lafayette, who visited New Orleans in 1825 as part of his tour of the United States, their organization was still undermanned. John Mercier, their new commander, explained to the celebrated visitor that he had just received his command, that they had been unorganized for some time, and were now attempting to reorganize.[43]

Jackson, who was seeking the presidency in 1828, accepted an invitation of the legislature to return to New Orleans to help celebrate the festivities in honor of the famous battle. He returned and was officially acclaimed as the hero of New Orleans. In the celebration of the battle of January 8, it is likely that some colored veterans marched, as reference is made to the gallant veterans of 1814 and 1815, but who they were or how many is not known. Certainly, no full-strength organization appeared, for by now the reaction against the free Negroes had begun in Louisiana. However, even in 1831 a memorial to the Governor from officers of the First Brigade urging a new militia law noted the peculiarly heterogeneous population of Louisiana and suggested placing arms in the hands of all free men whose interest was identified with the state and who were ready to defend it at all costs at anytime.[44]

It is quite understandable that the colored militia would fade out in the turmoil of the slavery controversy. What is less immediately clear is why the colored leaders permitted their militia, for whose recognition they had struggled so long prior to the war and whose continuance was encouraged afterwards by white officials, to decline in such a manner. Disappointment at not receiving a fuller measure of political and civil rights, such as voting and holding office, was only part of the answer, as was the loss of friends and members of the corps through aging and death.

To these must be added two larger and more compelling influences. One was the general unpopularity of the militia, which developed in Louisiana at the time as part of the national pattern, and the other was the economic prosperity which followed in the state in wake of the war. These were interrelated and both affected the free men of color and their organization.

After the war, the militia movement throughout the entire United States underwent a decline. Americans were simply not enthusiastic toward the militia in peacetime. Congress was aware of this and was seeking corrective measures. The same thing was happening in Louisiana. Four governors—Claiborne in 1816, Villeré in 1818, Robertson in 1823, and Roman in 1831—each had officially noted the disorganized state of the militia and consistently urged improvement.[45] Newspapers also took up the problem.[46] Although remedial legislation was passed in 1818, 1820, 1826, and 1829, these laws were only amendatory and failed to solve the basic problem.[47] With little exception militia duty remained oppressive to the rank and file, including the Negroes in Louisiana. And if their experience with Jackson after the battle did not intensify their feelings against the military, it certainly added nothing to its popularity.

Simultaneous with the development of indifference to the militia, significant commercial and agricultural changes occurred in the state. In 1815 the Fulton-Livingstone steamboat monopoly on the Mississippi was broken and the increasing river traffic was opened to all steam boats. Two years later, the introduction of ribbon cane, a sugar species, which ripened earlier and withstood more cold weather than other types, extended sugar cultivation to the parishes of the southwestern part of Louisiana. Sugar was now ground by steam power. A few years later, the refinement of sugar was improved by the use of the vacuum pan process. These changes were accompanied by a great influx of population as part of the westward movement. Louisiana experienced a great boom with the focal point in New Orleans. In 1840 this city ranked second in commerce in the United States and indeed, fourth throughout the world. In population it was outranked only by New York, Philadelphia, and Baltimore.

For the colored veterans, most of whom were already established as skilled craftsmen or small businessmen, this economic upsurge brought unprecedented opportunities for profitable employment and rendered militia duty all the more irksome. By 1820 former officers like Ferdinand Lioteau, Charles Porée, Jean Dolliole, and Baltazare Demozeillier were all busy as cabinetmakers. Carpenters like Pierre Badille, Noel Bonrepaux, Joseph Cabaret, John B. Coffie, Louis St. Martin, Louis Hazeur, Norbert Fortier, and Antoine Escot who had served with the colored militia, had no difficulty in plying their trade. Bricklayers like Vincent Cubidon, builders like François Boisdoire, and coopers like Noel Carrière had little if any slack time. This was equally true of tailors like Joseph Camps, Firmin Christopher, Barthelemy and Antoine Populus, just as it was for shoemakers like Basil Brion, François Duval, Francis Diez, and Maurice and Vincent Populus. Some veterans like Brion, who made shoes for ladies, and Populus, who was a merchant tailor, were specialists. Maurice and Vincent Populus, officers of the outfit from the earliest days, had a number of shoemaking shops, one at 108, another at 123, and a third at 153 Bourbon Street, an important business street of old New Orleans.[48]

Grocerymen included old veterans like Felix Delille, Etienne Lareau, Vitall Lanna, Jean Pierre, Louis Jean, Gilbert Beaulieu, and Louis St. Amand. The last two specialized in fowl. By 1828 some veterans like Detterville Bonseigneur, Joseph Medsingue, Nicholas Joly, and François Escoffier were tavern owners, while Joseph Camps was a coffeehouse proprietor.[49] Of these Delille, Camps, and St. Amand held licenses to retail spirituous liquor in quantities of pints and upwards. Certain individuals like the famous Joseph Savary and Isidore Honoré appeared more than once as bondsmen for tavern keepers and storekeepers who sold liquor. Colored veterans were more interested in taking advantage of the growing economic opportunities and had little or no time for the militia.

In one respect it was just as well that the free men of color permitted their militia to pass in this manner. They were caught in the bitter controversy between the forces of slavery and freedom and their very existence was threatened. It took all their energy to maintain status as free men, let alone as free colored militiamen. What happened was not astonishing. Westward migration and the economic boom in Louisiana not only attracted a large number of free people of both races to the state, but also introduced an increasingly large number of slaves to meet the ever-growing demand for labor on the docks at New Orleans and the plantations of the sugar parishes.

The result was soon obvious—the number of nonwhites came to exceed the whites. Such a condition, due mainly to the migration of Negroes from the Caribbean prior to 1819, was reflected in the census of 1810 when Negroes comprised 55.2 percent of the total population of the state. This proportion had declined to 51.8 percent in 1820, but by 1830 had risen to an all time high of 58.5 percent.[50] In other words, at that time there were 141,208 Negroes to each 100,000 whites.

Governor A. B. Roman, in his address opening the extra session of the legislature in 1831, called attention to this population disparity as well as to possible repercussions from the Nat Turner insurrection.[51] The danger of slave revolts, always frightening, became all the more imminent with this insurrection and the rise of the abolitionist movement, with its possibility of recruitment in Louisiana from the free Negroes and liberal whites.

Slaves had already attempted a revolt in March, 1829, just forty miles above New Orleans, and only speedy action on the part of the authorities prevented serious damage. Two of the leaders were tried and executed. But federal reinforcements at Baton Rouge were readied and offered to the governor of Louisiana on account of the "disquietude exhibited by the authorities and inhabitants" there caused by the "insurrectionary spirit maintained by the black population." [52] Although help was not accepted at the time there was no doubt that the need of a strong militia then became more urgent.

Louisiana immediately turned her attention to a security program and within the next few years enacted a series of measures designed to secure the slavery institution, eliminate the population disproportion, and establish a new militia. Accordingly, on April 1, 1829, by legislative enactment, slaves above twelve years of age could not be introduced into the state unless their owners or persons responsible for them presented a certificate of good moral character for each slave.[53] This certificate, which was to be formally executed before a court of record and deposited with the parish judge, had to show that the slave had never been guilty or convicted of any crime, did not run away, had not been accused of conspiracy or insurrection, nor had resided in any state or territory during time of conspiracy or insurrection.

Early in the following year, a comprehensive law was passed concerning the free people of color.[54] One section prevented free people of color from entering Louisiana after 1830. The only exceptions were seamen who could stay no longer than thirty days unless they were ill. This was to be carefully verified, and upon recovery they were required to leave immediately. Another section forced all free Negroes who had entered the state since January 1, 1825, to leave Louisiana within sixty days. This forced migration was based on a former territorial law of April 14, 1807, which forbade the migration of free people of color to the state.

A third feature of the act required all persons who had come into the state between the adoption of the state constitution in 1812 and 1825 to formally enroll themselves in registers maintained by the parish in which they resided or, in the office of the mayor of New Orleans. A final provision of the act restricted the freedom of speech by prohibiting communication of any kind whatsoever by white and free people of color which tended in any way to cause unrest among the slaves or free people, or to cause the latter to forget their status as far as the position of the majority race was concerned. These acts were to be enforced with stringency. Provisions were made for the removal and trial of officers who might be derelict in their duty of prosecution.[55]

Although the free colored people who comprised the group of veterans of the War of 1812 were not included within the legislation requiring either migration or registration, there is no doubt that they were otherwise affected. Their friends and relatives were involved and they themselves did not escape the restriction on freedom of speech. Already deprived of the ballot and now unable to agitate for political equality and other rights of citizens, their outlook was not bright.

Against this local background the new militia bill of 1834 was enacted.[56] But apart from reflecting the slavery controversy and the reaction against the free people of color and other conditions cited, it also sought to meet the demands of the War Department. One of these requirements, based on the law of 1792 which specified that the militia be composed of citizens, had by 1823 been interpreted to apply to the majority group exclusively, even though congressional acts of 1811, 1812, and 1814 which raised troops for the war contained no racial restrictions.[57]

The result in Louisiana where the slave controversy had become heated was a foregone conclusion. In the new law the word "white" was retained as it had been in the state law of 1812, but at the same time it repealed all other legislation heretofore passed concerning the militia.[58] This, of course, meant that the supplementary legislation setting up the Battalion of Chosen Men of Color in 1812 was repealed and thereupon the colored militia officially came to an end. But the outfit was already dying from natural causes abetted by economic materialism and the slavery controversy. This act only officially marked its demise. Failure to include the colored corps in subsequent militia acts prior to the Civil War confirmed the finality of the passing of the battalion.[59]

Death spared some of the old leaders any remorse which they might have felt at the passing of the corps. Louis Simon, a captain in the original Battalion of Chosen Men of Color, died in 1832.[60] He had not only remained active in the corps after the Battle of New Orleans but had led in signing the address to Governor Claiborne which offered the service of the colored militia to the new American government. By 1826, Captain Charles Forneret and Captain Ferdinand Lioteau were gone. Within a few years after the passage of the militia law other old leaders died. Prominent among these was Noel Carrière, a second generation officer of the colored militia, who died in 1835.[61]

Louisiana, through her program of security which became more strict as slave plots increased and the war approached, was able to reduce the disparity between the two races. From 1840 on, the percentage of Negroes in Louisiana population declined considerably and the proportion between the two races became more equalized. At that time the Negroes were 55 percent of the total population of the state.[62] This percentage fell to 50.7 by 1850 and to 49.5 by 1860. The number of free Negroes which had increased from 16,710 in 1830 to 25,502 in 1840, declined to 17,642 by 1850 and leveled off showing 18,647 in 1860.[63]

Even though such factors as deaths and births are included in these figures, there is no doubt that the free colored people left the state in considerable numbers after 1840. Some went to other parts of the United States where they occasionally passed the color line. Others, perhaps the largest portion, left Louisiana for such places as Haiti, where they had been especially invited and made welcome, and to Cuba, Mexico, Canada, and France.[64] In these areas, they neither had a language barrier nor found acculturation difficult.

Some old veterans sent their children abroad. An outstanding example of this is afforded by the famous dramatist Victor Séjour, son of Victor Séjour, former quartermaster in Daquin's battalion and proprietor of a drycleaning establishment in New Orleans. The elder Séjour persuaded his son to seek his fortune in Paris in 1836.

After completing his education, young Victor entered the literary circles of Paris with his ode in 1841 "La Retour of Napoleon." In 1844 he staged his first drama at the *Theatre-Français* and soon gained popularity as a playwright through some twenty productions which followed. Counting among friends such famous writers as the Dumas and Victor Hugo, he became, for a while, private secretary to Louis Napoleon. Of his plays only one had an American theme. This was "Les Volontiers de 1814," a drama in five acts and fourteen tableaux which featured the Louisiana colored volunteers, of which his father was one, in the Battle of New Orleans.[65] This play was presented in 1862 in the *Theatre-Français* and received a favorable press, thus extending the glory of the colored militia overseas by way of the stage.

While some of the colored veterans left New Orleans, the majority did not leave their home. Not only did age deter them. More important was the fact that the legislation concerning residence and emigration of the free colored people did not apply to them as has been indicated. Their military service was an important factor in their immunity from these laws.

Of the Negro veterans remaining in New Orleans, many drew themselves together in such social and benevolent associations as *La Societe des Artisans*, an organization of free colored mechanics incorporated in 1834. Meetings of this organization afforded its members a sounding board for literary expression and secret criticism of the power structure in New Orleans as well as for consideration of the society's regular business. The elder Sejour was a member. At one of its meetings, young Sejour read his first poem and received encouragement.

It is not unlikely that the free man of color, writing under the pseudonym Hippolyte Castra, recited his *"La Campagne de 1814–1815"* before this society.

Precisely when (before 1840) Castra, who claimed service on the firing line with Jackson in the ranks of the free men of color, became sufficiently overwhelmed by righteous indignation to compose his piece is not known. Nor is it certain whether it was perfected by Castra at the outset, or refined on the possible occasion of being presented to the colored society mentioned, or by Rodolph Desdunes who may have first published it in 1911 in his *Nos Hommes and Notre Histoire*.[66] Because of its subversive nature, it was said to have been handed down by word of mouth. Indeed, it is impossible to identify the author inasmuch as no such name appears on either the rolls of Lacoste's or Daquin's battalions. A suggestive name, Hipolyte Lafargue, is listed in the latter organization in Captain Lefevre company. It is more likely, however, that the author, whoever he may have been, for obvious reasons was writing under a pen name.

But there is no doubt as to the author's message. The poem, five stanzas of eight verses in French, praises the men of color on the battlefield, relates how all the soldiers, white and colored, were treated as heroes and fraternized together immediately after the battle, then reveals the disillusionment and bitterness of the colored men who subsequently felt the sting of race prejudice, persecution, and rejection. It is the only one of the many Afro-French poems of a protest nature extant in New Orleans at the time. It represents the nearest expression of regret at the passing of the colored militia corps and the plight of the free people of color.

Translated it reads:

The Campaign of 1814–15

I remember that, one day, during my childhood,
A beautiful morning, my mother, while sighing,
Said to me: "Child, emblem of innocence,
"You do not know the future that awaits thee.
"You believe that you see your country under this beautiful sky
"Renounce thy error, my tender child,
"And believe above all your beloved mother. . . .
"Here, thou art but an object of scorn."

Ten years later, upon our vast frontiers,
One heard the English cannon,
And then these words: "Come, let us conquer, my brothers,
"We were all born of Louisiana blood."
At these sweet words, and embracing my mother,
I followed you, repeating your cries,
Not thinking, in my pursuit of battle,
That I was but an object of scorn.

Arriving upon the field of battle,
I fought like a brave warrior;
Neither the bullets nor the shrapnel,
Could ever fill me with fear.
I fought with great valor
With the hope of serving my country,
Not thinking that for recompense
I would be the object of scorn.

After having gained the victory,
In this terrible and glorious combat,
All of you shared a drink with me
And called me a valiant soldier.
And I, without regret, and with a sincere heart,
Helas! I drank, believing you to be my friends,
Not thinking, in my fleeting joy
That I was but an object of scorn.

But today I sigh sadly
Because I perceive a change in you;
I no longer see that gracious smile
Which showed itself, in other times, so often

Upon your honeyed lips.
Have you become my enemies?
Ah! I see it in your fierce looks,
I am but an object of your scorn.

Although the colored corps was no longer heard from in a military capacity, and restrictions against the free people of color increased as the Civil War approached, the Negro veterans were by no means forgotten. The two addresses which Jackson had made before the battle were broadcast far and wide. John Greenleaf Whittier, in the *National Era* in 1847, referred to the second proclamation as "the highest compliment ever paid by a military chieftain to his soldiers." [67] Robert C. Winthrop, member of the House of Representatives from Massachusetts, not only extolled these troops in Congress in September, 1850, but in his zeal referred to the second speech of Jackson as being given after the battle instead of before.[68] In so doing, he inadvertently contributed, and possibly originated, an honest error which for many years resounded throughout the halls of Congress and elsewhere whenever reference was made concerning contributions of the Negro race to America. William C. Nell, pioneer Negro pamphleteer, helped to perpetuate the fame of these colored troops by printing the speeches in full in his *Services of Colored Americans in the War of 1776 and 1812* which was published in several editions at home and in Canada beginning in 1851.[69]

Of more immediate significance, however, were the tangible rewards, benefits, and honors which the veterans received. These took the form of pensions from the state, followed by bounty land warrants from the federal government, and finally honors again from Louisiana. There was one exception to this: Alexis Andry [private, Captain Demazelliere's Company] who had been blinded in the battle of the eighth, was awarded a pension by the federal government as of January 6, 1815.[70]

The Louisiana general assembly, in its first session after the War of 1812, enacted a law providing for the relief of persons wounded, and of widows and legitimate minor children of those killed in action.[71] Section four specifically extended the measure to free men of color and seamen. Amounts to be paid were to equal the soldier's pay while in service and were to extend from the day of casualty to the last day of the next legislative session. Pensions were subject to renewal. Accordingly, pensions were paid to the minor children of Morne Jesse, Fraise

Colomnie, and Joachim, colored soldiers of Daquin's battalion who died as a result of military action.

By special enactment, the relief of certain fathers, whose sole support had been their veteran sons, was provided for. This resulted from a petition which Charles Savary, father of Ensign Belton who was mortally wounded, was fortunate in getting Joseph Rouffignac, a sympathizer, to sponsor.[72] The measure passed by the legislature February 6, 1815, provided that the dependent, Savary, should receive from the state, eight dollars per month, the sum his son would have been entitled to in active service.[73] Payments were to be made quarterly. At least two other free men of color, Peter Valery and Jousin Reynier, received similar benefits on account of the death of their sons from the war.[74]

In 1819 the famous Major Joseph Savary, who had performed so heroically on the battlefield and who had been instrumental in raising the second battalion of colored volunteers, was awarded a pension of thirty dollars a month.[75] This ran for five years, after which it was extended for another four years. This was probably the highest pension Louisiana paid to any of its veterans of the War of 1812 at that time. Certainly it was the highest paid a Negro ex-soldier and unquestionably reflected the high esteem in which Savary was held by the people of the state—he was Louisiana's hero.

As time passed, age and need overtook other colored veterans or their survivors who applied for and received pensions. Some of the more popular of these, and the years their names first appeared on the state pension rolls, were: Vincent Populus, 1831, former second major of Lacoste's battalion; 1835, the widow of Louis Simon, former captain; Jean Baptiste Hardy, 1836, former captain; Isidore McCarthy Honoré, 1847, former lieutenant; Pierre Dupart, 1848, former sergeant; and Louis Hazeur, 1850, former senior musician.[76] Each of these received pensions at the regular rate of eight dollars a month, except Hardy who was awarded the same amount until 1836 when he was paid fifteen dollars. This he received until 1845 when his allotment was increased to twenty-five dollars.[77] This was the second highest award to these veterans. Pensioner Hardy was eighty years of age in 1836, possibly the oldest living Negro veteran.

Although the state pension act was modified in 1852 and 1853 in order to eliminate those veterans who had not been actually on the firing line, their survivors and those who were not in necessitous circumstances,[78] nevertheless, deserving colored veterans or their survivors continued on the pension rolls inasmuch as both battalions had served on the firing line. Their retention in the file was facilitated by an Association of Colored Veterans of 1814 and 1815 of New Orleans which was incorporated by the state in 1853.[79]

This colored association, composed of thirty-one charter members headed by Barthelemy Populus, former first lieutenant and adjutant of Lacoste's Battalion of Free Men of Color, was active in helping claimants who encountered difficulty in proving eligibility because of old age, illiteracy, or ignorance of the English language, or loss of credentials. While mainly charitable, this veterans' organization also kept alive the memory of the Battle of New Orleans. Its members rendered significant services not only in assisting veterans and their survivors in qualifying for benefits but also by aiding them in sickness and death.

Meanwhile, just about the time the pension rolls were undergoing revision, the federal government made provisions whereby rights to bounty lands were extended to the veterans of the War of 1812. This was done by a series of liberalizing land acts: one of 1850 entitled veterans of one month's service to forty acres in the public domain; that of 1852 amended the former to include any troops from any state or territory serving since 1812; and that of 1855 which entitled any soldier to 160 acres who had served fourteen days or more in any war in which the United States had engaged since 1790 and whose discharge was honorable.[80]

Almost immediately a brisk business in bounty land warrants developed in New Orleans. Enterprising businessmen who became particularly associated with bounty land claims of the colored veterans and their survivors included: William Clarke, George Dearing, Jr., George Palfrey, William Wilder, and Barthelemy Populus.[81] It will be recalled that the latter, the only Negro in the group, was a founder of the colored veterans' association and a former officer in Lacoste's outfit. So well organized did the business of securing and transferring land warrants become, that exploitation is at times suggested. This was largely untrue, however; what gave dispatch to this business was the ready cash market for land warrants.

Indeed, it is quite possible that the founders of the veterans association had the business of bounty land warrants in mind when they organized. In the summer of 1853, Wilder made a trip to Washington on behalf of those colored veterans who thought they were eligible for bounty land. The *Evening Star* of Washington advised the government to proceed with care in this matter. The *Daily Picayune* of New Orleans, however, answered that the claims were legitimate and that Wilder had the necessary information to substantiate them.[82]

Altogether, no less than 178 veterans of the Louisiana battalions of free men of color who served in the War of 1812 or their survivors applied for and received bounty land warrants from the federal government.[83] Most of these warrants were for 1850 and qualified the holder for forty acres. But a number of veterans or their heirs who were living in 1855, such as Louis Séjour, Barthelemy Populus, and Jean Bonseigneur, received warrants for the full amount of 160 acres.

Almost invariably, the Negro veterans or their survivors sold their warrants for bounty land to prospective easterners who planned to settle in the west. The veterans seldom knew or met the prospective settlers inasmuch as the entire transaction was arranged and consummated by land agents who had offices or contacts in New Orleans and Washington for that purpose. Although evidence of the amounts of money received by the veterans for their warrants is unavailable, the distribution of original assignees or locators by place reveals settlements in at least sixteen states and territories. Included were not only states of the old Northwest, such as Michigan and Illinois, but the California and Oregon territories in the far West.

Although the legislation providing bounty land to the colored veterans of Louisiana and others who did not previously qualify was not passed until 1850, and even though the colored veterans did not settle on their land grants, the legislation was nevertheless important. This was quite apart from its revenue feature. It was a redemption of the pledge made by Jackson to the free men of color in his first speech when he invited them to answer the call of their country and join him in the defense of New Orleans. It was a further manifestation of the government's policy of equal treatment to its veterans regardless of color.

In the ten-year period before the Civil War, the colored veterans were also honored by Louisiana through becoming a fixed part of the celebrations of the battle of January 8, 1815, which were then occurring annually. This was rather significant, for apart from pensions it had been a long time since the colored veterans as a group had received any public honor from the state.

The last occasion of any real importance in which they had participated was the laying of the cornerstone at Chalmette in 1840 at the dedication of Jackson's Monument to commemorate the battle of January 8, 1815. Jackson, by that time stooped with age, had participated in the ceremony and had expressed a wish to see the representatives of these colored troops. This was arranged and a large number of the colored veterans officially called on him at his hotel where he graciously received them.

General Plauché presented them as "the brave soldiers who fought in defense of the country under the orders of Majors Lacoste and Daquin and who now wished to pay their respects and shake the hand of their General as a token of gratitude." [84]

It was a deeply emotional moment for both Jackson and the veterans as they reminisced momentarily between handshakes over their common experience of twenty-five years earlier.

But in 1851 they were in the parade celebrating the battle of the eighth by special invitation of the authorities. Ninety free colored veterans marched in the center, according to the *Daily Picayune,* which was most enthusiastic over their participation and gave it considerable coverage. This was the first time in which they so participated in the annual rejoicing over the victory. The honor was long overdue, for the paper asked rhetorically: "Who more than they deserve the thanks of the country and the gratitude of the succeeding generations? Who rallied with more alacrity in response to the summons of danger? Who endured the hardships of the camp, or faced with greater courage the perils of the fight?" Indeed, they were the most interesting portion of the pageant "making an impression on every observer and eliciting unqualified approbation" as they marched by in a steady though slow cadence.

The paper then paid a glowing tribute to the free Negro population of New Orleans of which the veterans were a part. Not only were they a peaceable, orderly, respectable people, many of whom owned large amounts of property, but also they were a people with strong ties to New Orleans and Louisiana that could not be easily broken. The paper concluded in the same high vein, that "while they may be certain that insubordination will be promptly punished, deserving action will always be met with their due reward in the esteem and gratitude of the community." [85]

The colored veterans were flattered at such eulogistic praise. To some like the sensitive poet Hippolyte Castra, it may have been a dream deferred. To others like the record-minded adjutant Barthelemy Populus it was good to be rediscovered, except for one possible reservation. He might have liked the paper to go further and remind the public that the loyalty of the Negro to New Orleans and Louisiana had continued since 1729, shortly after the city was founded. Then slaves received their freedom for military service to the French and soon after became organized into a colored militia which had defended the city and province on every occasion when it became threatened by internal or external foe. The Battle of New Orleans, though climactic, was but one episode in the history of the colored militia's defense of New Orleans which stretched over almost a century. But Populus may have expected too much.

The paper had wrought well. After all, it was not primarily concerned with history. Too, it had possibly kindled the loyalty of the younger generations of free Negroes for another crisis looming on the horizon.

Nor did the praiseworthy account escape certain free Negroes of the North. The *Pennsylvania Freeman,* an abolitionist newspaper, not only reported it in full but used it as a lesson worthy of Northern emulation and as a rebuke to the North for its prejudice. As to the former, the paper called on all "who fear danger in the nation from the presence in it of a colored population to read and ponder it." They could quickly realize how colored freemen acted when fully protected by law and in possession of all their rights. The editor reminded the North that free Negroes there were also devoted to the safety and welfare of their country, in spite of the injustices they had received. Instead of this being publicized, however, as in New Orleans, the paper charged, it was concealed in the false and malicious statements against the injured race.

The paper then severely indicted the North with the "incident narrated is also a burning rebuke from a slave holding community to the vulgar (N) egro-hatred of the North, which drives the worthy colored men from popular processions, parades, schools, churches, and the so-called 'respectable avocations of life.' " [86]

Impressive as the *Pennsylvania Freeman* article was, the newspaper could hardly have been unmindful that Louisiana's free colored veterans, despite their uniqueness, did not entirely escape proscription. But there was no doubt that attitudes concerning them had shifted since 1850. When the militia committee of the legislature presented the memorial for organization of the veterans, it referred to the men in laudatory terms. It said the "conduct of the free colored population of Louisiana during the invasion of the State by the British Army in

1814–1815 entitles them to the gratitude and respect of every Louisianian, and they, the committee, believe it is the duty of the legislature as it will no doubt be its pleasure to grant the very reasonable prayer." [87]

The colored veterans continued to gather accolades. They were included in the order of procession and festivities for other years. Especially significant were those of 1856, 1859, and 1860. The first was the occasion of the presentation of C. Mills's famous equestrian statue of Jackson in New Orleans' Jackson Park.[88] Medals commemorating the event were distributed to the veterans at this time. The second event honored Lieutenant General Winfield Scott, hero of the War with Mexico.[89] It was quite an affair. General Henry W. Palfrey entertained about twenty-five of the colored veterans at his residence following the ceremonies for the visiting hero.

But the parade of January 8, 1860, according to the *Commercial Bulletin,* was the largest and most brilliant.[90] The colored veterans, as usual, appeared near the center of the parade but this time because of their age they rode in carriages. The celebration that year also included imposing civic and military ceremonies on Sunday in Jackson Square and, as a final feature, a procession to St. Louis Cathedral for the *Te Deum.* In addition, Jordan B. Noble, Jackson's famous drummer, was honored at the dinner for the veterans that day at the St. Charles Hotel.

Noble had not only remained in New Orleans after the war but had associated with the free people of color into whose group he had married. He subsequently became one of their leaders. At the same time he retained his connection with the military. As drummer with Louisiana troops, he served in the Seminole War in Florida, 1836, and then in the War with Mexico, 1846. His was the distinction, of which he was very proud, of having served as drummer in three of his nation's wars.[91]

When called on to make remarks on this occasion, he was well received as usual. Applause and cheers frequently interrupted his short speech, the gist of which was that he was ready to serve his country again as he had done before in New Orleans, Florida, and Mexico. On the same day a special medal for service rendered in the month of December, 1814, and on the eighth of January, 1815, in the Battle of New Orleans was publicly presented to Noble at the request of Major General Winfield Scott, who was present.[92]

At some point in that festive, crowded, yet ominous, weekend—for secession and the Civil War were near—Noble would repeat his long drum roll. But his long beat, which he had given in many concerts before, this time had a special kind of significance. It symbolized taps for all colored soldiers who had defended Louisiana since 1729. Along with the *Te Deum* sung at St. Louis Cathedral it marked "finished" to a chapter in the antebellum period of American history in which Louisiana Negro troops played a prominent role.

NOTES

CHAPTER I

1 Andrew Jackson's Letters and Orders, Letterbook G, September 21, 1814 (MS in Andrew Jackson Papers, Library of Congress), 157–58. Hereinafter cited as Jackson Letterbook G.

2 François-Xavier Martin, *The History of Louisiana From the Earliest Period* (New Orleans: James A. Gresham, 1882), 158; Charles Gayarré, *History of Louisiana* (New Orleans: F. F. Hansell and Brothers, 1903), I, 454; Dunbar Rowland and A. G. Sanders (eds. and trans.), *Mississippi Provincial Archives* (Jackson: Mississippi Department of Archives and History, 1927), I, 55 n 1. The number of slaves is estimated. Martin gives 1,800 for 1728 and Gayarré cites 2,500 for 1731.

3 Elizabeth Donnan, *Documents Illustrative of the History of the Slave Trade to America,* (Washington: Carnegie Institution of Washington, 1931), IV, 639.

4 "Memoir on Louisiana [by Bienville]" in Rowland and Sanders, *Mississippi Provincial Archives,* III, 523.

5 Joe Gray Taylor, *Negro Slavery in Louisiana* (Baton Rouge: Louisiana Historical Association, 1963), 9.

6 Code Noir ou Édit du Roy Servant de Règlement Pour le gouvernement et l'Administration de la justice, Police discipline et le commerce des esclaves Nègres dans la Province et Colonie de la Louisiane donné a Versailles au mois de Mars 1724 (Transcripts of the Archives Nationales Colonies, Paris, in the Library of Congress, A, 22: 119–28v. These transcripts hereinafter cited as LC ANC). See also Gayarré, *History of Louisiana,* I, 531–40.

7 Antoine Simon Le Page du Pratz, *The History of Louisiana . . .* (London: T. Becket and P. A. de Hondt, 1763), II, 260–64.

8 Périer and De la Chaise to the Directors of the Company of the Indies, November 3, 1728, in Rowland and Sanders, *Mississippi Provincial Archives,* II, 599.

9 Le Page du Pratz, *The History of Louisiana*, II, 260–64.

10 Périer to Maurepas, March 18, 1730, in Rowland and Sanders, *Mississippi Provincial Archives*, I, 71–72; Périer to Maurepas, December 5, 1729, *ibid.*, 54; Diron d'Artaguette to Maurepas, March 20, 1730, *ibid.*, 76–77.

11 Périer to the Abbé Raguet, April 25, 1727, in Rowland and Sanders *Mississippi Provincial Archives*, II, 542; Périer and De la Chaise to the Directors of the Company of the Indies, April 22, 1727, *ibid.*, 532.

12 Périer to Maurepas, December 5, 1729, in Rowland and Sanders, *Mississippi Provincial Archives*, I, 55.

13 Périer to Maurepas, April 10, 1730, with account of massacre written March 18, 1730, in Rowland and Sanders, *Mississippi Provincial Archives*, I, 67.

14 "Memorial of M. De la Chaise to the Councillors of the Superior Council of the Province of Louisiana," *Louisiana Historical Quarterly*, I (January, 1918), 132–33.

15 Périer to Maurepas, March 18, 1730, in Rowland and Sanders, *Mississippi Provincial Archives*, I, 64.

16 *Ibid.*, 67.

17 Dumont, "Memoir," in Benjamin French (ed. and comp.), *Historical Collections of Louisiana* . . . (New York: Wiley and Putnam, 1853), V, 81; Le Page du Pratz, *History of Louisiana*, I, 153; Périer to Maurepas, March 18, 1730, in Rowland and Sanders, *Mississippi Provincial Archives*, I, 67.

18 Périer to Maurepas, March 18, 1730, in Rowland and Sanders, *Mississippi Provincial Archives*, I, 64, 68–70.

19 "Data Concerning the Natchez Massacre," *Louisiana Historical Quarterly*, I (January, 1918) 126–31; Lusser to Maurepas with "Journal of the journey that I made in the Choctaw Nation by order of M. Périer, beginning on January 12, 1730 and lasting until March 23, of the same year," in Rowland and Sanders, *Mississippi Provincial Archives*, I, 81–113. In this account, Father Souel's Negro is said to have been killed with his master.

20 "Memorial of M. De la Chaise," *Louisiana Historical Quarterly*, I (January, 1918), 132–33.

21 "Records of the Superior Council," *Louisiana Historical Quarterly*, IV (October, 1921), 512–13.

22 "Proposition to Free Negroes for Military Merit by Attorney General Fleuriau," *ibid.*, 524.

23 *Negro Dicou (Ticou) vs. D'Auseville*, in Helen T. Catterall (ed.), *Judicial Cases Concerning American Slavery and the Negro* (Washington: Carnegie Institution of Washington, 1926), III, 410.

24 D'Artaguette to Maurepas, in Rowland and Sanders, *Mississippi Provincial Archives*, I, 78.

25 Le Page du Pratz, *The History of Louisiana*, I, 131–33. See also Dumont, "Memoir," in French, *Historical Collections of Louisiana*, V, 99–100.

26 Gayarré, *History of Louisiana*, I, 446; Martin, *The History of Louisiana*, 171.

27   Le Page du Pratz, *The History of Louisiana,* I, 131–33.
28   Dumont, "Memoir," in French, *Historical Collections of Louisiana,* V, 101.
29   1731 Enterprises de Guerre, Relations de la defaite des Natchez par M. De Périer commandant General a la Louisiane (LC ANC, C13A, 13: 39).
30   *Ibid.*
31   King [Louis XV] to Bienville, February 2, 1732, in Rowland and Sanders, *Mississippi Provincial Archives,* III, 540–41.
32   LC ANC, B, 43: 310v.
33   Bienville to Maurepas, September 30, 1734, in Rowland and Sanders, *Mississippi Provincial Archives,* I, 243–44.
34   *Ibid.,* 273.
35   "Narrative of the War Against the Chickasaws," in Rowland and Sanders, *Mississippi Provincial Archives,* I, 316.
36   Bienville to Maurepas, June 28, 1736, *ibid.,* 299; LC ANC, C13A, 21: 191.
37   Bienville to Maurepas, June 28, 1736, in Rowland and Sanders, *Mississippi Provincial Archives,* I, 305–306.
38   Dumont, "Memoir," in French, *Historical Collections of Louisiana,* V, 111.
39   "Narrative of the War Against the Chickasaws," in Rowland and Sanders, *Mississippi Provincial Archives,* I, 318–19, and 319n.
40   Dumont, "Memoir," in French, *Historical Collections of Louisiana,* V, 111; 1731 Recensement des habitations le long du fleuve Mississippi (LC ANC, G1, 464: [26]–27v). Simon, the colored officer, the first to be mentioned, is listed in the census of the plantation along the Mississippi taken in 1731 as *Simon Nègre Libre* who owned a plantation below the Tchoupitoulas.
41   Report to the King, in Rowland and Sanders, *Mississippi Provincial Archives,* I, 379–80.
42   Bienville to Maurepas, October 12, 1739, *ibid.,* 390.
43   Marc de Villiers du Terrage, *Les Dernières Années de la Louisiane Français, Le Chevalier de Kerlérec D'Abbadie-Aubry Laussat,* ed. E. Guilmoto (Paris: Librarie Orientale et Americaine, 1904), 22.
44   Bienville to Maurepas, August 30, 1739 (LC ANC, C13A, 24: 86). Report to the King, in Rowland and Sanders, *Mississippi Provincial Archives,* I, 386.
45   Martin, *The History of Louisiana,* 307.
46   From Bienville, June 1, 1740, in Rowland and Sanders, *Mississippi Provincial Archives,* I, 428–31.

CHAPTER II

1   Catterall, *Judicial Cases Concerning American Slavery,* III, 612.

2 *Ibid.*

3 Lyle N. McAlister, "The Reorganization of the Army of New Spain, 1763–1766," *Hispanic American Historical Review*, XXXIII (February, 1953), 12, 14–16; Jacobo de la Pezuela, *Historia de la Isla de Cuba* (Madrid: Bailly-Balliere, 1868–78), III, 2–25.

4 D. Joaquín Rodríguez San Pedro, *Legislación Ultramarina Concorda y Anotoda* (Madrid: Señores, Viota Y Vincente, 1865–69), II, 666.

5 Bucareli to Arriaga, July 6, 1769, in Lawrence Kinnaird (ed.), *Spain in the Mississippi Valley, 1765–1794: The Revolutionary Period, 1765–1781*, Vol. II of the *Annual Report of the American Historical Association for the Year 1945* (Washington: Government Printing Office, 1945), 88.

6 *Ibid.*, 88, 196.

7 Registre Institute Libertés á la Nouvelle Orléans le 15, février 1770, O'Reilly (MS on microfilm, Library of Congress).

8 Kinnaird, *Spain in the Mississippi Valley*, II, 290.

9 John Caughey, *Bernardo de Gálvez in Louisiana, 1776–1783* (Berkeley: University of California Press, 1934), 61; Josef De Galvez to Navarro, August 29, 1779, in Kinnaird, *Spain in the Mississippi Valley*, II, 355–57.

10 *Suplemento a la Gazeta de Madrid*, January 14, 1780, translated in the *Louisiana Historical Quarterly*, XV (July, 1932), 472–73.

11 *Ibid.*, 473–77.

12 *Suplemento a la Gazeta de Madrid*, 14 de Enero de 1780 (Original in Government Publication Division, Library of Congress), 39.

13 *Ibid.*, 42.

14 *Carrière* vs *Tixerant*, in Catterall, *Judicial Cases Concerning American Slavery*, III, 417.

15 Libro primero de Matrimonios de Negros y Mulatos de la Parroquia e St. Luis y la Nueva Orleáns en 137 folios de principio en 20 enero a 1777 y a Cuba en (y sigue esta el 29 Julio de 1830), March 19, 1804 (MS in St. Louis Cathedral, New Orleans).

16 Registre des actes de Inhumation des Personnes de Couleur libres et Catholices pour Église Cathédrale et Pariossiale de St. Louis de la Ville et Paroissi de la Nouvelle Orléans dans l'Etat de la Louisiane, aux Etats-Unis d'Amérique, Troisième Livre, July 1, 1835 (MS in St. Louis Cathedral, New Orleans).

17 "Diario que yo D. Bernardo de Gálvez, Brigadier de los Reales, Exercitos, Gobernador de la Provincia de la Luisiana, y engargado por S. M. de la expedicion contra Penzacola y la Mobila formo de los acaecimientos que occurren en ella," *Suplemento a la Gazeta de Madrid*, 20 Junio de 1780 (Original in Government Publication Division of Congress), 435–51.

18 Archivo General de Indias, Papelas de Cuba, Seville, Spain, (hereinafter cited as AGI PC), Legajo 184a.

19 "Diario de las Operaciones de la Expedición contra la Plaza de Penzacola concluia por las armes de S. M. Catolicia baxo los ordenes del Mariscal D. Bernardo de Gálvez, Penzacola 12 Mayo 1781," translated in the *Louisiana Historical Quarterly*, I (January, 1917), 44–48.

20 Kinnaird, *Spain in the Mississippi Valley*, II, 421.

21 Caroline Maude Burson, *The Stewardship of Don Esteban Miró, 1782–1792: A Study of Louisiana Based Largely on Documents in New Orleans* (New Orleans: American Printing Company, 1940), 102.

22 "Diario de las Operaciones de la Expedición contra la Plaza de Penzacola," 74; Burson, *The Stewardship of Don Esteban Miró*, 42.

23 *Gazeta de Madrid*, 21 Agosto de 1781 (Original in Government Publication Division, Library of Congress), II, 679; A. P. Nasatir (ed.), "Government Employees and Salaries in Spanish Louisiana," *Louisiana Historical Quarterly*, XXIX (October, 1946), 924.

24 AGI PC, Legajo 184a.

25 Kinnaird, *Spain in the Mississippi Valley*, II, 428–29.

26 Albert Phelps, *American Commonwealths; Louisiana: A Record of Expansion* (Boston: Houghton, Mifflin and Company, 1905), 148.

27 Burson, *The Stewardship of Don Esteban Miró*, 113. See also Records and Deliberations of the Cabildo (Typescript translation in New Orleans Public Library, hereinafter cited as Cabildo Books), Minutes for May 28, 1784.

28 Burson, *The Stewardship of Don Esteban Miró*, 113–17. See also Cabildo Books, Minutes for June 4, 1784.

29 Cabildo Books, Minutes for June 25, 1784.

30 *Ibid.*, Minutes for July 30, 1784.

31 Miscellaneous Spanish and French documents from December 23, 1769, to December 12, 1800 (Typescript translation in New Orleans Public Library), I, Nos. 175 and 176, pp. 101–103.

32 *Ibid.*

33 Archivo General de Indias, Papelas de Cuba, Seville, Spain (Photostats in Library of Congress, hereinafter cited as LC AGI PC), Legajo 2354, No. 129 (520–21). See also [Translation of] Messages of Francisco Luis Hector, El Baron de Carondelet, Sixth Governor of Louisiana, 1792–1797, Louisiana State Works Progress Administration Project, 1937–41 (Typescript in the National Archives, hereinafter cited as Carondelet Messages) XI, 280–81. See also map "City of New Orleans, Its Fortifications and Environs in 1798" in Martin, *The History of Louisiana*, following page 412.

34 LC AGI, Legajo 1441, No. 113 [433]–(434); Carondelet Messages, I, 372.

35 LC AGI, Legajo 1441, No. 113 (434); Carondelet Messages, I, 372–73.

36 LC AGI, Legajo 1441, No. 231 (894); Carondelet Messages, II, 135.

37 AGI PC, Legajo 184a.

38 LC AGI, Legajo 2353, [unnumbered letter] (108–13); Carondelet Messages, X, 65–67.

39 LC AGI PC, Legajo 2354, No. 129 (523); Carondelet Messages, XI, 281.

40 Gayarré, *History of Louisiana*, III, 354–55.

41 *Ibid.*; LC AGI PC, Legajo 1443 B, No. 732 (431–53); Carondelet Messages, V, 352–61.

42 Cabildo Books, Minutes for May 2, 1795.

43 *Ibid.*; LC AGI PC, Legajo 1447, No. 135½ (742–54); Carondelet Messages, IX, 209–14. For Carondelet's complete investigation of the con-

spiracy, see LC AGI PC, Legajo 153 A, No. 140 (284–435) ; Carondelet Messages, II, 220–74.

44 LC AGI PC, Legajo 1447, No. 140 (907) ; Carondelet Messages, IX, 222.
45 Burson, *The Stewardship of Don Esteban Miró*, 123 n 107.
46 LC AGI PC, Legajo 1443 A, No. 484 (59) ; Legajo 1447, No. 108 (524) ; Legajo 1444, No. 897 (397) ; Carondelet Messages, IV, 229; IX, 127; VI, 216.
47 Burson, *The Stewardship of Don Esteban Miró*, 104.
48 See Bailly's deposition as witness in the Batture case of October 16, 1807, involving Edward Livingstone in *Louisiana Historical Quarterly*, XXIII (July, 1940), 706–709.
49 "The Defenses of New Orleans in 1797," from the original in the Collection of J. W. Crusat, New Orleans, translated in *Publications of the Louisiana Historical Society*, I, Pt. 3, pp. 35–39.
50 AGI PC, Legajo 184a.
51 AGI PC, Legajo 179, No. 7 (1–3) .
52 Secret Instructions for the Captain-General of Louisiana Approved by the First Consul, in James A. Robertson (ed.) , *Louisiana Under the Rule of Spain, France, and the United States of America, 1785–1807* (Cleveland: Arthur H. Clark Company, 1911) , I, 369.
53 *Ibid.*, 361 n155.
54 Laussat to Decrès, July 18, 1803, in Robertson, *Louisiana Under the Rule of Spain*, II, 44.
55 *Ibid.*
56 *Ibid.*, 43.
57 Gayarré, *History of Louisiana*, III, 605–606.
58 *Ibid.*, 606.

CHAPTER III

1 William C. C. Claiborne to James A. Madison, December 27, 1803, General Records of the Department of State, Territorial Papers, Orleans (MS in Record Group 59, National Archives) .
2 *Ibid.*
3 Benjamin Morgan to Chandler Price, August 7, 1803 in Clarence E. Carter (ed.) , *The Territory of Orleans, 1803–1812*, Vol. IX of the *Territorial Papers of the United States* (Washington: Government Printing Office, 1940) , 6–7.
4 *Ibid.*
5 *Ibid.*
6 Claiborne to Henry Dearborn, June 22, 1804, in Dunbar Rowland (ed.) , *Letterbooks of W. C. C. Claiborne, 1801–1816* (Jackson: Mississippi Department of Archives and History, 1917) , II, 217–18, hereinafter cited as *Claiborne's Letterbooks*.

7 Libro primero de Matrimonios de Negros y Mulatos, March 19, 1804 (MS in St. Louis Cathedral, New Orleans).

8 Claiborne to Madison, January 17, 1804, Negro militiamen's address enclosed (MS in Record Group 59, National Archives).

9 *Ibid.*

10 *Ibid.*

11 *Senate Executive Documents*, 41st Cong., 3rd Sess., No. 36, 276.

12 Claiborne to Jefferson, September 29, 1803 (MS in Record Group 59, National Archives).

13 James Wilkinson to Dearborn, December 21, 1803 in Carter, *The Territory of Orleans*, 139.

14 Wilkinson to Dearborn, January 11, 1804, *ibid.*, 159.

15 *Ibid.*, 160.

16 Claiborne to Madison, January 17, 1804 (MS in Record Group 59, National Archives).

17 *Ibid.*

18 Dearborn to Claiborne, February 20, 1804, in Records of the Office of the Secretary of War (MS in Record Group 107, National Archives).

19 Claiborne to Dearborn, June 9, 1804, in Rowland, *Claiborne's Letterbooks*, II, 199–200.

20 Claiborne to Dearborn, June 22, 1804, *ibid.*

21 *Ibid.*

22 James Sterret to Nathaniel Evans, June 23, 1804, in Nathaniel Evans Papers, 1794–1807, Louisiana State University Department of Archives, Baton Rouge.

23 Claiborne to Madison, July 3, 1804 (MS in Record Group 59, National Archives).

24 *Ibid.*

25 Claiborne to Madison, July 5, 1804 (MS in Record Group 59, National Archives).

26 Claiborne to Madison, July 12, 1804 (MS in Record Group 59, National Archives).

27 Carter, *The Territory of Orleans*, 561.

28 *Louisiana Gazette*, January 29, 1805.

29 Statement of Stephen, a Free Negro, to Governor Claiborne, January 24, 1806 (MS in Record Group 59, National Archives).

30 *Ibid.*

31 Claiborne to Madison, January 24, 1806 (MS in Record Group 59, National Archives).

32 Libro primero de Matrimonios de Negros y Mulatos, 22 A, No. 3, December 12, 1805 (MS in St. Louis Cathedral, New Orleans).

33 Speech of Governor Claiborne to the Two Houses, January 13, 1807, in Rowland, *Claiborne's Letterbooks*, IV, 92–94.

34 *Ibid.*

35 General Orders of Governor Claiborne, December 16, 1806, to January 23, 1807 (MS in Record Group 107, National Archives).

36 *Annals of Ninth Congress, Second Session* (Washington: Gales and Seaton, 1852), 215.

37 Claiborne to Jefferson, June 12, 1807, with enclosures, in the Papers of Thomas Jefferson (Library of Congress).

38 *Ibid.*

39 *Ibid.*

40 Census of New Orleans, 1803, sent by Daniel Clark, Consul of New Orleans to the American Government, August 17, 1803 (MS in Record Group 59, National Archives).

41 Matthew Flannery (comp.), *New Orleans in 1805: A Directory and a Census Together with Resolutions Authorizing Same now Printed for the First Time* (New Orleans: Pelican Gallery, 1936), 107.

42 Claiborne to Madison, July 12, 1804 (MS in Record Group 59, National Archives).

43 *Acts Passed at the First Session of the First Legislature of the Territory of Orleans, 1806,* p. 128.

44 *Acts Passed at the Second Session of the First Legislature of the Territory of Orleans, 1807,* pp. 180–82.

45 Luiz M. Perez, "French Refugees to New Orleans in 1809," *Publications of the Southern History Association,* IX (September, 1905), 293–96.

46 Maurice Rogers to Claiborne, April 19, 1809, enclosed in Claiborne to Smith, May 20, 1809 (MS in Record Group 59, National Archives).

47 Mather to Claiborne, July 18, 1809, enclosed in Claiborne to Smith, July 20, 1809 (MS in Record Group 59, National Archives).

48 Mather to Claiborne, August 7, 1809, enclosed in Claiborne to Smith, August 9, 1809 (MS in Record Group 59, National Archives).

49 Extract of letter to mayor of the City of New Orleans, March 28, 1810, to His Excellency William C. C. Claiborne, Governor of the Territory of Orleans, enclosed in Claiborne to Smith, March 30, 1810 (MS in Record Group 59, National Archives).

50 Claiborne to Rogers, August 4, 1809, enclosed in Claiborne to Smith, November 12, 1809 (MS in Record Group 59, National Archives).

51 Claiborne to Savage, November 10, 1809, enclosed in Claiborne to Smith, November 12, 1809 (MS in Record Group 59, National Archives).

52 Smith to Claiborne, September 12, 1809 (MS in Record Group 59, National Archives).

53 Third Census, 1810 Population, Louisiana, Orleans Territory (MS photostat in Record Group 29, National Archives), 245.

54 *Ibid.,* 233.

55 Manuel Andry to Claiborne, January 11, 1811; also enclosure to Claiborne from *Courier de la Louisiana,* January 12, 1811, all enclosed in Claiborne to Smith, January 12, 1811 (MS in Record Group 59, National Archives).

56 Wade Hampton to Secretary of War, January 16, 1811, in Carter, *The Territory of Orleans,* 917–19.

57 *Ibid.*

58 Pardon by William Charles Cole Claiborne, Governor of the Territory of Orleans, in Rowland, *Claiborne's Letterbooks,* V, 198–99.

59 Claiborne to the Secretary of State, January 14, 1811, *ibid.,* 100.

60 Claiborne to Major St. Amand and Colonel Andre, January 14, 1811, in
    Rowland, *Claiborne's Letterbooks,* IV, 99.
61 Answer to the Legislative Council and of the House of Representatives,
    January 31, 1811, *ibid.,* 127–28, 131.
62 *Acts Passed at the Second Session of the Third Legislature of the Terri-
    tory of Orleans, Begun and Held in the City of New Orleans, January
    23, 1811* p. 196.
63 Message of Claiborne to the Territorial Legislative Council and House of
    Representatives, February 25, 1811, in Rowland, *Claiborne's Letterbooks,*
    V, 163.
64 *Ibid.*
65 Claiborne to Monroe, July 20, 1812, *ibid.,* VI, 132.
66 *Journal of the House of Representatives of the State of Louisiana, First
    Session, First Legislature, 27 July, New Orleans, 1812,* pp. 4, 33.
67 *Ibid.,* 34.
68 *Ibid.,* 46–51.
69 *Ibid.,* 54, 69.
70 *Ibid.,* 74–75, 80.
71 Claiborne to Monroe, July 20, 1812 in Rowland, *Claiborne's Letterbooks,*
    VI, 132.
72 *Acts Passed at the First Session of the First Legislature of the State of
    Louisiana, Begun and Held in the City of New Orleans, July 27, 1812,*
    p. 72.
73 Military Pension File of Isidore Honoré (MS in Record Group 15, Na-
    tional Archives).
74 *Acts Passed at the Second Session of the First Legislature of the State of
    Louisiana, Begun and Held in the City of New Orleans, November 3,
    1812,* pp. 40–84.
75 *Ibid., passim.*

CHAPTER IV

1 Henry Adams, *The Second Administration of James Madison, 1813–
   1817* (New York: Charles Scribner's Sons, 1891), 313.
2 G. R. Gleig, *Narrative of the Campaigns of the British Army at Washington, Baltimore, and New Orleans Under Generals Ross, Pakenham,
   and Lambert in the Years 1814 and 1815* (London: John Murray,
   1847), 242–48.
3 Charles B. Brooks, *The Siege of New Orleans* (Seattle: University of
   Washington Press, 1961), 23–25; Jane Lucas De Grummond, *The
   Baratarians and the Battle of New Orleans* (Baton Rouge: Louisiana
   State University Press, 1961), 30–31; Major A. Lacarriere Latour, *Historical Memoir of the War in West Florida and Louisiana in 1814–
   1815 with an Atlas* (Philadelphia: John Conrad and Company, 1816), 6.

4 Brooks, *The Siege of New Orleans*, 70.
5 Records of the Office of the Secretary of War, Military Book, No. 7, 200–201 (MS in Record Group 107, National Archives). See also Records of the Office of the Adjutant General, Register of Appointments, Nominations and Confirmations, 1812–25 (MS in Record Group 94, National Archives), 205. See Records of the U.S. Army Command, Post-Revolutionary Collection, 0124–0125 (MS in Record Group 98, National Archives), 86.
6 Andrew Jackson to Claiborne, July 21, 1814, Jackson Letterbook G, 9–10.
7 Jackson to Major General Thomas Pinckney, Commanding 6th Military District, August 4, 1814, Jackson Letterbook G, 31–33.
8 Claiborne to Jackson, August 8, 1814 (MS in Andrew Jackson Papers, Library of Congress, hereinafter cited as Jackson Papers.)
9 Claiborne to Jackson, August 12, 1814, *ibid.* See also John Spencer Bassett (ed.), *Correspondence of Andrew Jackson* (Washington: Carnegie Institution of Washington, 1933), VI, 436.
10 Claiborne to Jackson, August 12, 1814, in Jackson Papers.
11 *Ibid.*
12 Jackson to Claiborne, August 22, 1814, Jackson Letterbook G, 66–68.
13 Claiborne to Jackson, August 21, 1814, in Jackson Papers.
14 Militia General Orders, Headquarters, August 18, 1814, in *Louisiana Courier*, August 19, 1814.
15 Claiborne to Jackson, August 21, 1814, in Jackson Papers.
16 Claiborne to Jackson, August 24, 1814, *ibid.*
17 Committee of Safety to Jackson, September 18, 1814, *ibid.*
18 Claiborne to Jackson, September 20, 1814, *ibid.*
19 Latour, *The War in West Florida and Louisiana*, 84.
20 Jackson to John Armstrong, Secretary of War, September 17, 1814, Jackson Letterbook G, 130–31.
21 *Ibid.*
22 Jackson to Claiborne, September 21, 1814, Jackson Letterbook G, 152–53.
23 *Ibid.*
24 *Ibid.*
25 *Ibid.*
26 Claiborne to Jackson, October 17, 1814, in Jackson Papers.
27 Claiborne to Jackson, October 28, 1814, in Rowland, *Claiborne's Letterbooks*, VI, 292–94.
28 Jackson Letterbook G. September 21, 1814, pp. 157–58.
29 *Ibid.*
30 *Ibid.*
31 *Ibid.*
32 Jackson to Claiborne, October 31, 1814, Jackson's Letters and Orders, Book H (MS in Andrew Jackson Papers, Library of Congress), 119, hereinafter cited as Jackson Letterbook H.
33 Claiborne to Jackson, November 4, 1814, in Jackson Papers.
34 Jackson to Monroe, December 2, 1814, Jackson Letterbook H, 151.
35 Jackson to Monroe, November 20, 1814, *ibid.*, 156–59.

36 Jackson to Monroe, December 10, 1814, *ibid.*, 152–53.
37 Benson Lossing, *The Pictorial Field Book of the War of 1812.* . . . (New York: Harper and Brothers, 1868), 1024–25; De Grummond, *The Baratarians,* 37–48.
38 Latour, *The War in West Florida and Louisiana,* 57–64.
39 Captain C. L. Humphrey to Colonel Butler, December 16, 1814, in Jackson Papers.
40 New Orleans *Tribune,* September 15, 1864.
41 Humphrey to Butler, December 16, 1814, in Jackson Papers.
42 Jackson Letterbook H, 167–72.
43 Jackson to Dusong, December 15, 1814, Jackson Letterbook H, 167.
44 See Muster Roll of Captain Ferdinand Lioteau (MS in Record Group 94, National Archives).
45 See Muster Rolls for each company arranged by captain's name, *ibid.*
46 See Muster Roll of Field Staff and Noncommissioned Staff Officers and Band of the First Battalion of Free Men of Color of the Militia of the State of Louisiana, *ibid.*
47 See Muster Roll of Captain Louis Simon, *ibid.* See Military Pension File of Joseph Frick, Private. (MS in Record Group 15, National Archives).
48 See Military Pension File of Barthelemy Populus (MS in Record Group 15, National Archives).
49 État General des campagnes de Vétérants Sous Mon Commandement (G. Depuy, Captain), in Jackson Papers.
50 Gayarré, *History of Louisiana,* IV, 406.
51 Printed copy of Jackson's Address in Jackson Papers, December 18, 1814.
52 *Ibid.*
53 See Muster Roll of each captain of the Second Battalion (MS in Record Group 94, National Archives).
54 See Muster Roll of the Field and Staff and Noncommissioned Staff Officers of the Battalion of Free Men of Color in the Militia of the State of Louisiana, Commanded by Major Daquin from 19 December, 1814, to 20 March, 1815 (MS in Record Group 94, National Archives).
55 See Muster Roll for each company arranged by captain's name (MS in Record Group 94, National Archives).
56 See Military Pension File of Jean Bonseigneur, Captain Lefevre's Company (MS in Record Group 15, National Archives).
57 Jackson to Claiborne, December 18, 1814 and Claiborne to Jackson, December 20, 1814, in Jackson Papers.
58 Robert Butler, Adjutant General to Captain Rivery, Department Commissary Purchases, December 21, 1814, Jackson Letterbook H, 183.
59 Gayarré, *History of Louisiana,* IV, 406. Bernard Marigny, "Reflections on the Campaign of General Andrew Jackson in Louisiana in 1814 and 1815," *Louisiana Historical Quarterly,* VI (January, 1923), 74.
60 Claiborne to Jackson, December 21, 1814, in Jackson Papers.
61 *Ibid.,* December 22, 1814.
62 Butler to Captain Ogden, December 22, 1814, Jackson Letterbook H, 186.
63 Jackson to Captain Humphrey, December 21, 1814, Jackson Letterbook H, 179.

CHAPTER V

1 Latour, *The War in West Florida and Louisiana*, 104.
2 *Ibid.*, 104.
3 Jackson to Monroe, December 27, 1814, in Bassett, *Correspondence of Andrew Jackson*, II, 126–27.
4 Andrew Jackson's personal account of the Battle of New Orleans (MS in Library of Congress).
5 See Military Pension File of Jordan B. Noble (MS in Record Group 15, National Archives); also exhibit in honor of, including drum, at the Cabildo, Louisiana State Museum, loan of Gasper Cusach, former president of Louisiana Historical Society.
6 Gleig, *Narrative of the Campaigns*, 288.
7 Jackson's personal account of the Battle of New Orleans.
8 *Ibid.*
9 John Eaton, *Memoirs of Andrew Jackson, Late Major General and Commander-in-Chief of the Southern Division of the Army of the United States* (Boston: Charles Ewer, 1828), 238–39.
10 *Ibid.*
11 *Ibid.*
12 Alexander Walker, *Jackson and New Orleans: An Authentic Narrative of the Memorable Achievements of the American Army, Under Andrew Jackson, Before New Orleans, in the Winter of 1814–15* (New York: J. C. Derby, 1856), 170–71; Latour, *The War in West Florida and Louisiana*, 95–96; Lossing, *Pictorial Field Book of the War of 1812. . . ,* p. 1030.
13 Latour, *The War in West Florida and Louisiana*, 96–97.
14 Jackson to Monroe, December 24, 1814, Jackson Letterbook H, 197.
15 Latour, *The War in West Florida and Louisiana*, 97.
16 *Ibid.*, 97–100.
17 Return of Casualties in the Army under the Command of General Keane in the Action with the Enemy near New Orleans, on the 23rd and 24th of December 1814; under the Command of Major General, the Honorable, Sir E. M. Pakenham between the 25th and 31st, December, 1814, between the 1st and 5th of January, 1815, and for the 8th of January, 1815; and for Major General Lambert between the 9th and 26th of January, 1815 (Library of Congress Photostats: Great Britain, London, Public Records Office, War Office 1), Vol. CXLI. Hereinafter cited as British Casualty Report.
18 Report of the Killed, Wounded, and Missing of the Army under the Command of Major General Andrew Jackson in the Action of the 23rd and 28th (of) December, 1814, and the 1st and 8th of January with the Enemy, in Jackson Papers, hereinafter cited as American Casualty Report.
19 Jackson to Monroe, December 24, 1814, in Bassett, *Correspondence of Andrew Jackson*, II, 126–27.
20 *Ibid.*
21 *Louisiana Courier*, July 13, 1818.

22 Jackson to Allen, Assistant Paymaster, Mobile, December 23, 1814, Jackson Letterbook H, 187–88.
23 *Ibid.*
24 Muster Roll of Captain Charles Forneret (MS in Record Group 94, National Archives).
25 Walker, *Jackson and New Orleans*, 195, 198–205, 208.
26 Lord Bathurst to Pakenham, October 24, 1814, in Public Records Office, War Office 6, Vol. II. See also Bathurst to Ross, October 5, 1814, *ibid.*
27 Latour, *The War in West Florida and Louisiana*, 114–15.
28 *Ibid.*, 115–16.
29 Jackson to Lacoste, December 25, 1814, Jackson Letterbook H, 193.
30 Latour, *The War in West Florida and Louisiana*, 115.
31 *Ibid.*, 117
32 *Ibid.*
33 De Grummond, *The Baratarians*, 104.
34 Brooks, *The Siege of New Orleans*, 200.
35 Latour, *The War in West Florida and Louisiana*, 122–26.
36 New Orleans *Tribune*, September 15, 1864.
37 Latour, *The War in West Florida and Louisiana*, 132.
38 Brooks, *The Siege of New Orleans*, 202.
39 British Casualty Report.
40 American Casualty Report.
41 *Ibid.*
42 Jackson to Monroe, January 2, 1815, in Bassett, *Correspondence of Andrew Jackson*, II, 130.
43 Gleig, *Narrative of the Campaigns*, 323–25; John H. Cooke, *A Narrative of Events in the South of France and of the Attack on New Orleans* (London: T. & W. Boone, 1835), 215–16.
44 Walker, *Jackson and New Orleans*, 310–12.
45 Military Pension File of Isidor Sandos (MS in Record Group 15, National Archives).
46 Latour, *The War in West Florida and Louisiana*, 147–49. See "Atlas Plate No. 7."
47 See Jackson to Adair, July 23, 1817, in Bassett, *Correspondence of Andrew Jackson*, II, 316; Latour, *The War in West Florida and Louisiana*, 152; Report of the Troops at Camp below New Orleans in the Action with Enemy on the 1st and 6th, in Jackson Papers. Latour's estimates are used inasmuch as they more nearly agree with Jackson's figures which are not given for individual units but for wings. Ross's are for units but for the day preceding the battle and exceed the figures of both Jackson and Latour.
48 Military Pension File of Jordan B. Noble (MS in Record Group 15, National Archives).
49 For Pakenham's troop disposition for the battle of the eighth which Keane forwarded to the Duke of Wellington, see Keane's "Journal of Operation Against New Orleans," in *Supplementary Dispatches and Correspondence, and Memoranda of Field Marshal Arthur Wellesley,*

Duke of Wellington, K. G., edited by his son, The Duke of Wellington (London: J. Murray, 1861), X, 399–403.

50 James Parton, *Life of Andrew Jackson* (Boston: Houghton, Mifflin and Company, 1887) , II, 189–93.

51 *Ibid.,* 194–95; Brooks, *The Siege of New Orleans,* 232.

52 Brooks, *The Siege of New Orleans,* 241, 251–52.

53 Jackson to Monroe, January 13, 1815, in Bassett (ed.) *Correspondence of Andrew Jackson,* II, 142–43. See also 143 n5 and American Casualty Report.

54 Latour, *The War in West Florida and Louisiana,* 244.

55 See Muster Roll of Captain Forneret (MS in Record Group 94, National Archives) ; Historical Notes on Fort St. Leon, especially prepared for the writer by Thomas Harrison, military historian, Jackson Barracks, New Orleans.

56 Walker, *Jackson and New Orleans,* 343–44. See Muster Roll of Captain Simon and American Casualty Report.

57 Walker, *Jackson and New Orleans,* 343–44.

58 *American Casualty Report;* Walker, *Jackson and New Orleans,* 343.

59 John S. Bassett (ed.), *"Major Howell Tatum's Journal While Acting Topographical Engineer to General Jackson Commanding the Seventh Military District"* (Northampton, Mass.: Smith College Studies in History, October, 1921–April, 1922) , VII, 130.

60 Colonel Ross's Casualty Report, in Jackson Papers.

61 Latour, *The War in West Florida and Louisiana,* 244, and Letter No. XXIX, Appendix, lx.

62 *Niles' Weekly Register,* February 11, 1815.

63 American Casualty Report.

64 Colonel Ross's Casualty Report, in Jackson Papers.

65 British Casualty Report.

66 Lossing, *Pictorial Field Book of the War of 1812. . . . ,* 1050.

67 Eaton, *Memoir of Andrew Jackson,* 255.

68 Gordon to Jackson, January 4, 1815, in Jackson Papers.

69 Gordon to Jackson, January 11, 1815, in Jackson Papers.

70 Major Gordon's Morning Report, January 18, 1815, in Jackson Papers.

71 Latour, *The War in West Florida and Louisiana,* 187–91, 196.

72 Military Pension File of Belton Savary (MS in Record Group 15, National Archives) .

73 See Muster Rolls of Captain Marcellin Gillot's Company; Captain Demozelliere's Company; Captain St. Martin's Company; Captain Lioteau's Company and Captain Forneret's Company (MS in Record 94, National Archives) .

CHAPTER VI

1 Jackson to the Reverend Mr. Dubourg, January 19, 1815, Jackson's Let-

ters and Orders, Book H (MS in Andrew Jackson Papers, Library of Congress), 228.

2 General Orders, By Command, The Adjutant General, 7th Military District, January 21, 1815, *Niles' Weekly Register.*

3 *Ibid.*

4 Admiral Cochrane to Rear Admiral Malcolm; Admiral Cochrane to Major General Lambert, February 17, 1815, in Public Records Office, War Office 1, Vol. CXLIII.

5 Colonel Young to Claiborne, February 1, 1815, Adjutant General's Book (Louisiana) February, 1815–February, 1827, on microfilm in Library of Congress.

6 Claiborne to Jackson, January 31, 1815, and Jackson to Claiborne, February 3, 1815, in Jackson Papers.

7 *Acts Passed at the First Session of the Second Legislature of the State of Louisiana, 1814–1815,* pp. 84–86.

8 Captain Bourgeau's Muster Roll, *Legion des France,* in Jackson Papers.

9 Major Louis Daquin to Brigadier General Robert McCausland, February 15, 1815, *ibid.*

10 *Ibid.*

11 Jackson to Colonel M. Arbuckle, March 5, 1815, Jackson's Letters and Orders, Book I (MS in Andrew Jackson Papers, Library of Congress hereinafter cited as Jackson Letterbook I.), 25. Writers have mistaken the ill-shaped S in the MS as L. A careful comparison with other S forms through the Letterbook leaves no doubt in the minds of the writers and Dr. Powell, formerly of the Manuscript Division of the Library of Congress, that the name intended is Savary.

12 Report of the Absentees from the Battalion of Majors Lacoste and Daquin, February 20, 1815, in Jackson Papers. Names are listed.

13 Daquin to McCausland, February 24, 1815, *ibid.*

14 Claiborne to Jackson, February 24, 1815, *ibid.*

15 Jackson to Claiborne, February 25, 1815, Jackson Letterbook I, 16.

16 Claiborne to Mur (ur) eau, February 24, 1815, in Rowland, *Claiborne's Letterbooks,* VI, 338–39.

17 Extract from General Order of February 28, 1815, in Bassett, *Correspondence of Andrew Jackson,* II, 181.

18 General Order of March 5, 1815, Adjutant General's Book (Louisiana), on microfilm in Library of Congress.

19 *Louisiana Courier,* March 3, 1815.

20 Jackson to Arbuckle, March 5, 1815, Jackson Letterbook I, 24.

21 Jackson to Peter Ogden, March 11, 1815, *ibid.,* 33–34.

22 Claiborne to the Secretary of State, March (undated) 1815, in Rowland, *Claiborne's Letterbooks,* VI, 344–45.

23 Jackson to Beale, March 6, 1815, Jackson Letterbook I, 27–28.

24 General Order of March 7, 1815, *ibid.,* 29–30.

25 Orders (Explanatory of Former Orders), March 14, 1815, in Jackson Papers.

26 Bassett, *Correspondence of Andrew Jackson,* II, 188–89, and 188 n 2.

27 General Order of March 14, 1815, *Niles' Weekly Register,* VIII, 124–25.

28 See Muster Rolls for each company arranged by captain's name (MS in Record Group 94, National Archives).

29 Payroll Records of a Company of Militia of Coloured Men Commanded by Captain Louis Simon in the Services of the United States from 16th December, 1814, to the 25th March, 1815 (MS in Record Group 94, National Archives).

30 Payroll for Major Populus and Major Savary, *ibid.*

31 See Payroll of individual companies (MS in Record Group 94, National Archives).

32 Discharge Certificate of William W. St. Leger (MS in Record Group 15, National Archives).

33 Discharge Certificate of Barthelemy Populus, *ibid.*

34 General Order of October 4, 1815, Adjutant General's Book (Louisiana) on microfilm in Library of Congress.

35 General Order, December 9, 1815, *ibid.*

36 Orders and Letters (Louisiana Military Historical Data Collection, Jackson Barracks, New Orleans), XLIX, 73.

37 *Ibid.*, L, 8.

38 General Order of September 16, 1816. Adjutant General's Book (Louisiana) on microfilm in Library of Congress.

39 Orders and Letters, XLIX, 83.

40 *Ibid.*, L, 25.

41 Order of March 28, 1818, Adjutant General's Book (Louisiana) on microfilm in Library of Congress.

42 After Special Order, March 14, 1825, *ibid.*

43 *Louisiana Courier*, April 19, 1825. See also, Orders and Letters, CCCXL, 124.

44 *Mercantile Advertiser*, July 11, 1831.

45 *Louisiana Courier*, September 8, 1816, and October 23, 1818; *Journal of the Senate, 1st Session, Sixth Legislature, State of Louisiana, New Orleans, January 7, 1823*, pp. 17–18; *Louisiana Advertiser*, February 2, 1831.

46 See *Louisiana Gazette*, July 17, 1818, December 5, 1822, October 10, 1825; *Louisiana Courier*, October 6, 1827.

47 Orders and Letters, CCCXL, 124.

48 John Adams Paxton, *The New Orleans Directory and Register Containing the Names, Possessions, and Persons in Business of the City and Suburbs; Notes on New Orleans with Useful Information* (New Orleans: Benjamin Levy, 1822). No page numbers given for names. Names arranged alphabetically.

49 Mayor's Office, Bond Book, City of Orleans, 1828, Bond Nos. 184, 170, 133, 265, 82 (MS in New Orleans Public Library).

50 U. S. Department of Commerce, Bureau of the Census, *Negro Population, 1790–1915* (Washington: U.S. Government Printing Office, 1918), 51, 62.

51 *Journal of the House of Representatives of the State of Louisiana, Extra Session, Tenth Legislature, 1831*, pp. 2–3.

52 Herbert Apetheker, *American Negro Slave Revolts* (New York: Columbia University Press, 1943), 283.

53 *Acts Passed at the First Session of the Ninth Legislature of the State of Louisiana, 1828–29,* pp. 38–50.

54 *Acts Passed at the Second Session of the Ninth Legislature of the State of Louisiana, 1830,* pp. 90–94, 96.

55 *Ibid.,* 94, and *Acts of Legislature, First Session, Ninth Legislature, 1828–29,* pp. 44–45.

56 *Acts Passed at the Second Session of the Eleventh Legislature of the State of Louisiana, 1833–1834,* pp. 143–67.

57 See Report of William Wirt, *Attorney General's Report in Executive Document, 26th Congress, 2nd Session,* 451–52.

58 *Acts Passed at the Second Session of the Eleventh Legislature of the State of Louisiana, 1833–1834,* pp. 143–67.

59 *Acts Passed at the Second Session of the Fifteenth Legislature of the State of Louisiana, 1841,* pp. 324–76. See subsequent acts.

60 Registre Obituaire des Personnes de Couleur Libres et Esclaves, November 13, 1832 (MS in St. Louis Cathedral, New Orleans).

61 Registre des actes de Inhumation des Personnes de Couleur Libres et Catholices, July 1, 1835 (MS in St. Louis Cathedral, New Orleans).

62 *Negro Population, 1790–1915,* 51.

63 *Ibid.,* 57.

64 New Orleans *Daily Picayune,* July 15, 1859; New Orleans *Daily True Delta,* June 21, 1859.

65 Edward Laroque Tinker, *Les Écrits de Langue Française en Louisiana au XIXe Siecle Essais Biographiques et Bibliographiques* (Paris: Librarie Ancienne Honoré Champion, 1932), 427–41; Charles Barthelemy Rousséve, *The Negro in Louisiana: Aspects of His History and His Literature* (New Orleans: Xavier University Press, 1937), 82–91.

66 Rodolphe L. Desdunnes, *Nos Hommes et Notre Histoire* (Montreal: Arbor et Dupont, 1911), 8–9.

67 *National Era,* July 22, 1847.

68 William Nell, *Services of the Colored Americans in the War of 1776 and 1812* (Philadelphia: A.M.E. Publishing House, 1894), 24. John Mercer Langston, congressman from Virginia, made this error in his speech before the Second Session, Forty-Second Congress. Quoted in Carter G. Woodson, *Negro Orators and Their Orations* (Washington: Associated Publishers, 1925), 389.

69 Nell, *Services of Colored Americans,* 25–26.

70 File of Alexis Andry (MS in Record Group 92, National Archives).

71 *Acts Passed at the First Session of the Second Legislature of the State of Louisiana, 1814–1815,* pp. 86–90.

72 *Journal of the House of Representatives During the First Session of the Second Legislature of the State of Louisiana, 1815,* p. 116.

73 *Acts Passed at the Second Session of the Second Legislature of the State of Louisiana, 1816,* p. 102.

74 *Ibid.*

75 *Acts Passed at the First Session of the Fourth Legislature of the State of Louisiana, 1819,* pp. 9–10; *Acts Passed by The First Session of the Sixth Legislature of the State of Louisiana, 1823,* p. 70.

76 *Acts Passed at the Extra Session of the Tenth Legislature of the State of Louisiana, 1831*, pp. 9–10; *Acts Passed at the First Session of the Twelfth Legislature of the State of Louisiana, 1835*, p. 229; *Acts Passed at the Second Session of the Twelfth Legislature of the State of Louisiana, 1836*, p. 192; *Acts Passed at the Second Session of the First Legislature of the State of Louisiana, 1847*, p. 84; *Acts Passed at the Second Session of the First Legislature of the State of Louisiana, 1847*, p. 99; *Acts Passed by the Third Legislature of the State of Louisiana, 1850*, p. 223.

77 *Acts Passed at the First Session of the Seventeenth Legislature of the State of Louisiana, 1845*, p. 59.

78 *Acts Passed by the Fourth Legislature of the State of Louisiana, 1852*, pp. 154–55; *Acts Passed by the First Legislature of the State of Louisiana, 1853*, pp. 262–68.

79 *Journal and Official Documents of the Senate of the State of Louisiana, 1853*, p. 50.

80 Henry C. Harmon, *A Manual of Pension Bounty, and Bounty Land Laws of the United States of America* (Washington: W. H. and O. H. Morrison, 1867), 54–57, 60–63.

81 New Orleans *Daily Picayune*, April 24, 1853.

82 Washington *Evening Star*, August 9, 1853, and August 17, 1853; New Orleans *Daily Picayune*, August 18, 1853.

83 Compiled from information in Military Bounty Land Files (MS in Record Group 49, National Archives).

84 *Louisiana Courier*, January 13, 1840.

85 New Orleans *Daily Picayune*, January 9, 1851.

86 *Pennsylvania Freeman*, March 10, 1851, quoted in William Nell, *Services of Colored Americans*, 26.

87 *Journal and Official Documents of the Senate of the State of Louisiana, 1853*, p. 50.

88 New Orleans *Daily Picayune*, February 10, 1856.

89 *Ibid.*, January 11, 1859.

90 New Orleans *Commercial Bulletin*, January 9, 1860.

91 Military Pension File of Jordan B. Noble (MS in Record Group 15, National Archives).

92 New Orleans *Commercial Bulletin*, January 9, 1860.

BIBLIOGRAPHY

Archival Records and Manuscripts

Unsurpassed in value for this study have been various record collections in the National Archives. Record Group 15, Records of the Veterans' Administration, and Record Group 49, Records of the General Land Office, contain an individual file for each veteran or survivor who applied for either a pension or disability benefit and bounty land respectively. Record Group 94, Records of the Office of the Adjutant General, includes the muster and pay-rolls for each company of free men of color. Record Group 107, Records of the Office of Secretary of War, is composed in part of correspondence from General Jackson and Governor Claiborne to that official of the Federal Government. In Record Group 98, Records of the United States Army, Post-Revolutionary Collection, are found fleeting pieces pertaining to General Jackson and his command of the Seventh Military District. Record Group 59, General Records of the Department of State, include the original letters, documents, and other communications of W. C. C. Claiborne while governor of Orleans Territory to the Secretary of State. These are in thirteen volumes and contain several items which have not been published.

Of equal significance have been collections in the Manuscript Division of the Library of Congress. Included are The Papers of Andrew Jackson which contain many orders, rosters, morning reports, casualty reports and other items of correspondence which have never been published. General Jackson's personal account of the Battle of New Orleans is also located here. Certain of the papers of Thomas Jefferson also shed light on the subject. In the same division are collections in photostats of the War Records of Great Britain's Public Records Office in London; in photostats and transcripts of the Papelas de Cuba in the Archivo General de Indias in Seville, Spain; and in transcripts of the Archives Nationales Colonies of France in Paris.

135

Each of these collections contains a wealth of information on different aspects of the subject. Among these, the Messages of Francisco Luis Hector, El Baron de Carondelet, Sixth Governor of Louisiana, 1792–97, have been translated as a Works Progress Administration Project in eleven typescript volumes, 1937–38, copies of which are in both the Library of Congress and the National Archives. The Adjutant's General Book, Louisiana, February, 1815–February, 1827, is on microfilm in the Library of Congress.

Legajo 184a of the Archivo General de Indias which contains commissions issued members of the colored militia is located in Seville.

Also of rare value have been the manuscripts in New Orleans and its vicinity. Folio volumes of the Registre des actes de Inhumation des Personnes de Couleur libres et Catholices pour Église Cathédrale et Paroissiale de St. Louis de la Ville et Paroissi de la Nouvelle Orléans dans l'Etat de la Louisiane, aux Etats-Unis d'Amérique; Registre Obituaire des Personnes de Couleur Libres et Esclaves; and Libro primero de Matrimonias des Negres y Mulatos of the parish of St. Louis and New Orleans, are among the priceless archives of Saint Louis Cathedral in New Orleans.

In the City Archives Room of New Orleans Public Library are: the Bond Book, City of New Orleans, 1828, from the Mayor's Office; Miscellaneous Spanish and French Documents from December 23, 1789 to December 12, 1806; and the Records and Deliberations of the Cabildo, (5 vols.) 1769–1803. Scattered throughout some of the typescript volumes of the Historical Military Data collection in Jackson Barracks is information concerning the battalions of free men of color. This is particularly true of Volumes 49 and 339 which contain orders and state pension lists, respectively, of the colored corps.

Gayarré's brief manuscript on the free men of color in Louisiana and their participation in the Battle of New Orleans and the Sterret letter mentioning the corps are among pertinent material in the Louisiana State University Department of Archives in Baton Rouge in the Charles E. Gayarré Collection and Henry Remy Papers, respectively.

The following printed works were indispensable:

Government Publications and Printed Documents

Acts Passed at the First Session of the First Legislature of the Territory of Orleans, 1806. New Orleans: Bradford and Anderson, 1807.

Acts Passed at the Second Session of the First Legislature of the Territory of Orleans, 1807. New Orleans: Bradford and Anderson. No publication date.

Acts Passed by the General Assembly of the State of Louisiana, 1812–79, various sessions, twenty-three vols. A separate volume was published for each session of the legislature. Each of the twenty-three volumes found useful was published in New Orleans with the exception of the one for 1830 which was published in Donaldsonville.

An Account of Louisiana, Being an Abstract of Documents, in the Offices of the Departments of State and of the Treasury. Philadelphia: William Duane, 1803.

Annals of Ninth Congress, Second Session. Washington: Gales and Seaton, 1852.

Executive Document of the Senate, No. 36, 41st Congress, 3rd Session. Washington: Government Printing Office, 1871.

Journal of the House of Representatives of the State of Louisiana, First Session, First Legislature, 1812. No publication data.

Journal of the House of Representatives of the State of Louisiana, Extra Session of Tenth Legislature. No publication data.

Journal of the House of Representatives of the State of Louisiana, First Session, Tenth Legislature. New Orleans: John Gibson, 1831.

Journal and Official Documents of the State of Louisiana, Session of 1853. New Orleans: La Sere, 1853.

Supplementary Despatches, Correspondence, and Memoranda of Field Marshal Arthur Wellesley, Duke of Wellington, K. G. Edited by His Son, the Duke of Wellington, 15 Vols. London: J. Murray, 1861.

U.S. Department of Commerce, Bureau of the Census, Negro Population 1790–1915. Washington: Washington Government Printing Office, 1918.

Books

Adams, Henry. *The Second Administration of James Madison, 1813–1817.* Vol. VIII of *History of the United States of America.* New York: Charles Scribner's Sons, 1891.

Apetheker, Herbert. *American Negro Slave Revolts.* New York: Columbia University Press, 1943.

Bassett, John Spencer (ed.). *Major Howell Tatum's Journal While Acting Topographical Engineer to General Jackson Commanding the Seventh Military District,* Smith College Studies in History, Vol. VII, Nos. 1, 2, and 3. Northampton, Mass., October, 1921, to April, 1922.

_____. *Correspondence of Andrew Jackson.* 7 Vols. Washington: Carnegie Institution of Washington, 1926–35.

Brooks, Charles B. *The Siege of New Orleans.* Seattle: University of Washington Press, 1961.

Burson, Caroline Maude. *The Stewardship of Don Esteban Miró, 1782–1792: A Study of Louisiana Based Largely on Documents in New Orleans.* New Orleans: American Printing Company, 1940.

Carter, Clarence Edwin (ed.). *The Territory of Orleans, 1803–1812.* Vol. IX of *The Territorial Papers of the United States.* Washington: Government Printing Office, 1940.

Catterall, Helen Tunncliff (ed.), *Cases from the Courts of Georgia, Florida, Alabama, Mississippi and Louisiana.* Vol. III of *Judicial Cases Concerning American Slavery and the Negro.* Washington: Carnegie Institution of Washington, 1932.

Caughey, John W. *Bernardo De Gálvez in Louisiana, 1776–1783.* Berkeley: University of California Press, 1934.

Cooke, John H. *A Narrative of Events in the South of France and of the Attack on New Orleans.* London: T. and W. Boone, 1835.

De Grummond, Jane L. *The Baratarians and the Battle of New Orleans.* Baton Rouge: Louisiana State University Press, 1961.

De la Pezuela, Jacobo. *Historia de la Isla Cuba.* 4 Vols. Madrid: Bailly-Balliere, 1868-1878.

Desdunes, Rodolphe L. *Nos Hommes et Notre Histoire.* Montreal: Arbor et Dupont, 1911.

Donnan, Elizabeth (ed.). *Documents Illustrative of the History of the Slave Trade to America.* 4 Vols. Washington: Carnegie Institution of Washington, 1935.

Du Pratz, Antoine Simon Le Page. *The History of Louisiana, or of the Western Parts of Virginia and Carolina: Containing a Description of the Countries that Lye on Both Sides of the River Mississippi: with an Account of the Settlements, Inhabitants, Soil, Climate, and Products. Translated from the French with Some Notes and Observation Relating to Our Colonies.* 2 Vols. London: T. Becket and P. A. de Hondt, 1763.

Du Terrage, Marc de Villiers. *Les Dernières Années de la Louisiane Français, Le Chevalier de Kerlérec, D'Abbadie-Aubry, Laussat.* Paris: Librarie Orientale et Americaine, 1904.

Eaton, John H. *Memoirs of Andrew Jackson, Late Major General and Commander in Chief of the Southern Division of the Army of the United States.* Compiled by a citizen. Boston: Charles Ewer, 1828.

Flannery, Matthew (for the City Council). *New Orleans in 1805: A Directory and a Census Together with Resolutions Authorizing Same Printed for the First Time from the Original Manuscript.* Facsimile. New Orleans: The Pelican Gallery, Inc., 1936.

French, Benjamin F. *Historical Collection of Louisiana, Embracing Translations of Many Rare and Valuable Documents Relating to the Civil and Political History of that State.* Compiled with Historical and Biographical Notes and an Introduction. 5 Vols. New York: Wiley T. Putnam, 1846-53.

Gayarré, Charles E. *History of Louisiana*. 4 Vols. New Orleans: F. F. Hansell and Bros., 1903.

Gleig, G. R. *Narrative of the Campaigns of the British Army at Washington, Baltimore, and New Orleans Under Generals Ross, Pakenham, and Lambert in the Years 1814 and 1815*. London: John Murray, 1847.

Harmon, Henry C. *A Manual of Pension Bounty and Bounty Land Laws of the United States of America: Embracing All the Laws under which Pensions, Bounties and Bounty Lands Are Now Granted*. Washington: W. H. and O. H. Morrison, 1867.

Kinnaird, Lawrence (ed.). *Spain in the Mississippi Valley, 1765-1794. The Revolutionary Period, 1765-1781*, Vol. II of *The Annual Report of the American Historical Association*. 4 Vols. Washington: United States Printing Office, 1945.

Latour, Major A. Lacarriere. *Historical Memoir of the War in West Florida and Louisiana in 1814-1815 with an Atlas*. Translated for the author by H. P. Nugent. Philadelphia: John Conrad and Company, 1816.

Lossing, Benson J. *The Pictorial Field-Book of the War of 1812; or Illustrations by Pen and Pencil of the History, Biography, Scenery, Relics and Traditions of the Last War for American Independence*. New York: Harper and Brothers, 1868.

Martin, François-Xavier *The History of Louisiana from the Earliest Period.* New Orleans: James A. Gresham, 1882.

Nell, William C. *Services of Colored Americans in the Wars of 1776 and 1812*. Philadelphia: A. M. E. Publishing House, 1894.

Parton, James. *Life of Andrew Jackson*. 3 Vols. Boston: Houghton, Mifflin and Company, 1887.

Paxton, John Adams. *The New Orleans Directory and Register Containing the Names, Possessions, and Persons in Business of the City and Suburbs; Notes on New Orleans with Useful Information*. New Orleans: Benjamin Levy, 1822.

Phelps, Albert. *American Commonwealths; Louisiana: A Record of Expansion*. Boston: Houghton, Mifflin and Company, 1905.

Robertson, James A. (ed.). *Louisiana under the Rule of Spain, France, and the United States, 1785-1807. Social, Economic, and Political Conditions Represented in the Louisiana Purchase as Portrayed in Hitherto Unpublished Contemporary Accounts by Dr. Paul Alliot and Various Spanish, French, English, and American Officials*. 2 Vols. Cleveland: Arthur H. Clark Company, 1911.

Rousseve, Charles B. *The Negro in Louisiana: Aspects of His History and His Literature*. New Orleans: Xavier University Press, 1937.

Rowland, Dunbar (ed.). *Letter Books of W. C. C. Claiborne, 1801-1816*. 6

Vols. Jackson: Mississippi Department of Archives and History, 1917.

Rowland, Dunbar and A. G. Sanders (eds.). *Mississippi Provincial Archives. Collected, Edited, and Translated by the Authors.* 3 Vols. Jackson: Mississippi Department of Archives and History, 1927–32.

San Pedro, Joaquín Rodríguez (et als). *Legislación Ultramarina Concordia y Anotada.* 16 Vols. Madrid: Señores, Viota y Vicente, 1865–69.

Taylor, Joe Gray. *Negro Slavery in Louisiana.* Baton Rouge: Louisiana Historical Association, 1963.

Tinker, Edward Laroque. *Les Écrits de Langue Française en Louisiane au XIXe Siècle; Essais Biographiques et Bibliographiques.* Paris: Librarie Ancienne Honoré Champion, 1932.

Walker, Alexander. *Jackson and New Orleans: An Authentic Narrative of the Memorable Achievements of the American Army.* New York: J. C. Derby, 1856.

Woodson, Carter G. *Negro Orators and Their Orations.* Washington: The Associated Publishers, 1925.

Periodicals

Journals, Pamphlets, and Gazettes

Gazeta de Madrid, 1779–81
Hispanic American Historical Review
Journal of Negro History
Journal of Southern History
London Gazette, for the year 1815
Louisiana Historical Quarterly
Niles' Weekly Register
Publications of the Louisiana Historical Society
Publications of the Southern Historical Association

Newspapers

Unless otherwise stated, papers were published in New Orleans.

Commercial Bulletin   *Louisiana Gazette*
Daily Picayune   *Mercantile Advertiser*
Daily True Delta   *Tribune*
Louisiana Advertiser   Washington *Evening Star*
Louisiana Courier   Washington *National Era*

INDEX

141

LOUISIANA STATE UNIVERSITY STUDIES

The Studies was established to publish the results of research by faculty members, staff, and graduate students of the University. Manuscripts of exceptional merit from sources other than aforementioned are considered for publication provided they deal with subjects of particular interest to Louisiana.

The Studies originally appeared as a unified series consisting of forty-two numbers, published between the years 1931 and 1941. In 1951 the Studies was reactivated, and is now being issued in the following series: Social Sciences, Humanities, Biological Sciences, Physical Sciences, and Coastal Studies. Other series may be established as the need arises.